ESS

Scotland

by
BARNABY ROGERSON

Barnaby Rogerson was born in Dumfermline
and finished his education at St Andrews. He has
written several guide books to the Islamic countries
of the Mediterranean. When not travelling Barnaby
builds follies.

Produced by AA Publishing

2

Written by Barnaby Rogerson
Verified by Barnaby Rogerson
Peace and Quiet section
by Paul Sterry
Original photography by Richard
Elliott

Revised second edition 1997
Reprinted 1995 (twice)
First published 1994

Edited, designed and produced by
AA Publishing.
© The Automobile Association
Maps © The Automobile Association

Distributed in the United Kingdom
by AA Publishing, Norfolk House,
Priestley Road, Basingstoke,
Hampshire, RG24 9NY.

A CIP catalogue record for this book
is available from the British Library.

ISBN 0 7495 1336 5

Country Distinguishing Signs

On some maps, international
distinguishing signs have been
used to indicate the location of
countries next to Scotland.
Thus:

(IRL) = Ireland

The contents of this publication are
believed correct at the time of
printing. Nevertheless, the publishers
cannot be held responsible for any
errors or omissions or for changes in
details given in this guide or for the
consequences of any reliance on the
information provided by the same.
Assessments of attractions, hotels,
restaurants and so forth are based
upon the author's own experience
and, therefore, descriptions given in
this guide necessarily contain an
element of subjective opinion which
may not reflect the publisher's
opinion or dictate a reader's own
experience on another occasion.
**We have tried to ensure accuracy
in this guide, but things do change
and we would be grateful if
readers would advise us of any
inaccuracies they may encounter.**

Published by AA Publishing, a
trading name of Automobile
Association Developments Limited,
whose registered office is Norfolk
House, Priestley Road, Basingstoke,
Hampshire, RG24 9NY.
Registered number 1878835.

Colour separation: BTB Colour
Repro, Whitchurch, Hampshire

Printed by: Printers S.R.L., Trento,
Italy

Front cover picture: *Eilean Donan
Castle*

This book employs a simple
rating system to help choose
which places to visit:

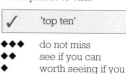

| ✓ | 'top ten' |

♦♦♦   do not miss
♦♦   see if you can
♦   worth seeing if you
      have time

Contents

Introduction and Background

INTRODUCTION

Scotland is not just a geographic location. It also exists in the minds of those who cherish images of highland cattle in mist-swept glens, of lone border towers standing beside hanging trees and of a hermit-like Celtic saint whose only friends are the wild otters.

These images, half cliché-half reality, mingle with the pibroch, the mournful droning lament of the bagpipes, the foredoomed but exhilarating adventures of Mary Queen of Scots and Bonnie Prince Charlie, the taste of whisky, the clear mountain air and the scent of the sea on golf courses and sandy beaches. It is this heady mixture that draws streams of appreciative visitors in a summer season that stretches over five months from May to September. And it is on these aspects that this guidebook dwells, addressing itself to a pleasure-seeking vacationer rather than a student concerned with socio-economic trends

Some awareness of present-day realities can only improve your holiday, however. Scotland is a nation with its own flag and coinage but it is no longer an independent state. Having fought long, hard and heroically to maintain its sovereignty, it surrendered it in a voluntary act of parliamentary union with England and Wales in 1707. The church, the legal and educational systems and local government were deliberately excluded from the provisions of the treaty, and remain proudly Scottish and different – if not better – to this

Whisky stills, where the wort is heated to give off the precious spirit

LOCATOR MAP

*Raw material for
Harris tweed –
dyed wool drying
in the sunshine*

day. The Union, with its in-built dominance by
the richer, more populous southern neighbour,
who was also the historic enemy, has never
been outstandingly popular but it has worked.
Scottish pride might be diminished by a
parliament that always sits in London, but the
region has so far gained financially, and
consistently provided more than its quota of
inspiring political leaders, generals and
financiers. Scottish nationalism has always
remained alive and fans itself up to a good
separatist heat once a generation. In the most
recent referendum, in 1979, the vote failed to
reach the necessary 40 per cent at which a
good measure of devolution would have taken
place. However, Scotland makes its
independence of spirit very clear. Its political
and social agendas are very different from
those of the rest of Britain, and Edinburgh and
Glasgow are perhaps more truly European
than any other British cities.

BACKGROUND

The Callanish stone circle, Lewis, is one of a series which fringe the Atlantic Coast from the Shetlands to Portugal

BACKGROUND

Prehistory and the Golden Age

The story of man in Scotland could not begin until the glaciers retreated from Northern Scotland some 12,000 years ago. They have scoured the rocks clean of any trace of earlier man here and the land mass is still rising in delayed relief at their passing. The first hunter-gatherers, in family groups seldom larger than 40, would have arrived in a virgin landscape filled with woods, marsh and wild game. They kept to the shellfish-rich coasts and were a transitory element in the landscape until the Neolithic revolution transformed mankind. It reached Scotland around 4000 BC to bring settled agriculture, stock breeding, permanent village communities and a vastly expanded population. It appears to have been a golden age of mankind and Scotland is littered with magnificent prehistoric relics, such as communal burial chambers and stone circles, that point to small communities of peaceful farmers with a very active spiritual life. The old civilisation shows signs of decay by around 1500 BC and was destroyed five hundred years later by armed warrior bands who introduced cruel slashing bronze swords, gorgeous golden ornaments, the curious circular dwellings called wheel-houses and the first hill-forts. They, like most of the early migrations into Scotland, came up the Irish Sea and used the stepping stones of the Hebrides to arrive in the central Highlands. The militant Celtic culture of this society was reinforced by the iron technology that accompanied a further wave of invaders around 600 BC. These new arrivals tended to build smaller hill-forts, of which some on the east coast have been vitrified (where rock has fused and glazed in intense heat), perhaps during the destruction of their timber-laced walls by fire.

Beyond the Frontier of the Roman Empire

The Romans, when they invaded the British Isles five hundred years later, were to call the people of Scotland the Picts. They never

More than 500 brochs were built between the first and fourth centuries AD. They worked as defensive structures until the enemy discovered that all you needed to do was throw lighted material into their middles, whereupon they acted like superefficient flues and were destroyed. This is Dun Troddan Broch, Glenelg

seriously contemplated the conquest of the whole of Scotland, which they knew as Caledonia, though the marching camps of the more enterprising generals, like Governor Agricola in the 1st century AD and the Emperor Septimius Severus in the 3rd century, can be traced deep into Scotland.

The military frontier that was originally sited across the Forth-Clyde valley (the Antonine Wall) was abandoned and replaced by Hadrian's Wall, whose remains stand just south of the existing Anglo-Scottish frontier. The Roman presence may have stimulated a demand for slaves, which might explain the oddity and frequency of certain 1st-century AD structures. These include *crannogs* (man-made islands in inland lochs reached on submerged stepping stones), *souterrains* (underground tunnel chambers), double-walled *broch* towers and the dry-stone, D-shaped fortlets known as *duns*, all of which were perhaps built to protect the Picts against slave raids.

BACKGROUND

Celtic cross – Port of Ness, Lewis

The Birth of Alba in the Dark Age

On to this indigenous culture three distinct outside groups imposed themselves in the 5th and 6th centuries. Boatloads of Anglo-Saxon tribes settled the southeast coast, the Gaelic-speaking Scotti of Ireland took the west coast while Romanised Celts advanced up from the south to establish the Kingdom of Strathclyde. Missionaries from the latter two cultures, represented by the great founding fathers like St Columba of Iona and St Ninian of Whithorn, gradually spread Christianity throughout the land and established a common identity. But the four-cornered struggle for dominance remained unresolved until the 8th century when Viking raids provided a common enemy that threatened to destroy them all. Faced with pagan settlers and recurring coastal raids, the remnants of the old kingdoms of the Picts, Angles and Scots united to form the kingdom of Alba under Kenneth MacAlpine in 843. Scone, a central inland settlement on the Tay, was the symbolic centre of this state, which slowly expanded into the unified Kingdom of Scotland. Strathclyde was absorbed in the 11th century.

A Quiet Cultural Revolution

In the late 11th century an influx of educated refugees brought the shared culture of Western Europe, complete with Roman law, Latin rites and Romanesque architecture, to the lowlands of Scotland. The Celtic Church and the oral Gaelic culture that formerly received the patronage of the royal court were submerged. Today, the glories of the old Irish-based monastic culture are recalled in thousands of place-names, dozens of fine stone crosses, but only a very few buildings.

The 12th and 13th centuries saw the emergence of an impressive series of Gothic abbeys and burghs, trading towns each with its own royal charter of liberties. Some of these towns still have a characteristic charm, with corbelled gables and broad red pantiles directly borrowed from the Low Countries. Many of the old burghs boasted wide central streets to hold markets, a mercat cross, a tolbooth tower which acted as both prison and town hall, a fine stone church and a harbour pier guarded by a castle.

The seal of Robert the Bruce

The Trouble is England: 1296–1328

The reigns of Alexander II and III, which stretched from 1214 to 1285, were the great age of Scottish medievalism but their achievements were nearly destroyed by English invasions in the next generation. Petty raids, invasion and counter-invasion had been a recurring theme of the border life for centuries but the period from 1296 to 1328 was a veritable struggle for national survival. The villain of the piece was Edward I of England, whose military ambitions had been forged in civil war and hardened by his successful conquest of Wales. When the heir of Scotland, Margaret the Maid of Norway, was tragically drowned while returning to her inheritance, he saw his chance to impose his lordship over the claims of Bruce and Balliol, the rival heirs. John Balliol was chosen king but soon grew disgusted at the underlying English control and, allying himself to France in 1295, he marched south. Edward's response was terrible: he ransacked Berwick before occupying Perth, Stirling and Edinburgh and as a symbol of his power sent the Stone of Scone (the ancient, venerated stone on which the Scottish kings were crowned) south to grace his throne at Westminster. John Balliol was deposed and the country was ruled by English officials backed up by garrisons. The Scottish lords acquiesced and it was left to William Wallace, a lowland commoner, to offer some resistance. Eventually, he trounced the English forces at the battle of Stirling Bridge in 1297. Edward I promptly raised a fresh army which destroyed Wallace's brave band at Falkirk the next year. Wallace remained at large until his betrayal and execution in 1305.

Robert the Bruce

The early career of Robert the Bruce, supported by the English, does not bear too close an examination. All this recedes into the background in 1306, when he had himself crowned at Scone and thereafter led the fight for independence. This proved a long, uphill struggle and he found himself at times with only a handful of supporters. It was during such a time that Bruce, in exile on Rathlin Island, off

*Highland scene –
Loch Tay*

the Irish coast, became entranced as a spider
attempted to sling its web over a beam,
achieving its aim only on the seventh attempt.
His spirits recovered at this image of the
rewards of perseverance and he relaunched
the guerrilla campaign which gradually
reduced the English hold over the country to a
few garrison towns. His campaign reached its
triumphant conclusion with the great victory
over the English at Bannockburn in 1314. The
war shifted south back to the familiar
battleground of the Borders before peace was
signed in 1328. The old hero king died the next
year of leprosy; his young son, David II,
inherited all of his father's enemies but few of
his strengths. His long reign was beset by
coups fomented by exiled nobles and an 11-
year period of hospitable captivity in London.
He was succeeded by his nephew Robert II,
the first of the Stewart dynasty. The Stewarts
were a Norman family settled in Scotland who
had risen to become hereditary High Stewards
and had then changed their surname from
FitzAlan to Stewart to reflect their status.

The Early Stewarts: 1371–1542

The rule of the Stewart dynasty is a recurring
Renaissance tale of *coups*, betrayals, sudden
murder and long-awaited revenge.
Throughout the 15th and 16th centuries a
succession of King Jameses, from I to V,
struggled against the influence of their over-
mighty nobility. Each painful advance in the
authority of the central government dissolved
with the death of a monarch, the effect of which
was often compounded by the near anarchy
associated with a child king. The soaring
fortified walls of the towerhouses of these times
give physical expression to such periods of
troubled politics, while their evolution from a
simple cube to an L or Z plan reveals the
corresponding extension of power of a local
noble family. The development of artillery and
a dependent alliance with France had allowed
the Scottish crown some measure of authority
by the 16th century. This strength and
confidence resulted in the Western Isles, and
the Orkneys and Shetlands being successfully
absorbed into the Scottish state.

Mary Queen of Scots

The Protestant Reformation and Mary Queen of Scots

The Protestant Reformation of the 16th century, for all its heroism and individual soul-searching, can also be read as just another faction fight among the nobility. James V, fortified by the practical support and strong faith of two French Catholic wives, refused to follow the example of his English neighbour and strengthen the crown by confiscating the lands of the Church. The nobility had no such scruples and began to look favourably upon the reformers and an expedient alliance with Protestant England. They deserted their monarch, and the weakened Scottish army was defeated at Solway Moss by the English in 1542. James, as he lay dying, heard that his wife had given birth to a girl.

The regency established to rule for the infant Queen Mary, from 1542 to 1561, at first achieved a near miraculous balance between Reformers and Catholics but that was soon ruined by the 'rough wooing' by England that began in 1544. Henry VIII despatched an army under the Earl of Hertford who repeatedly raided Scotland in an attempt to win the hand of Mary for the young Protestant heir of England. As a policy it was spectacularly unsuccessful and pushed Scotland further into the hands of the unpopular French-Catholic party. Cardinal Beaufort and the Queen Mother governed the country with the aid of French troops and a rash of heresy trials and public burnings. The Lords of the Congregation, as the leaders of the Protestant party styled themselves from 1557, aided by impassioned reformers like John Knox, the agents of Elizabeth I of England and genuine popular support in the towns, began to master Scotland. By 1560 they had pillaged the monasteries, deposed the regent, prohibited the mass and formally adopted the Geneva confession (the Swiss town was the centre for European Protestantism).

Into this maelstrom arrived the young widowed Queen Mary (who spelt her surname Stuart), whose Catholic faith, French education and marriage to a French king made her an object of suspicion to the triumphant Protestant

BACKGROUND

It's all peaceful enough now, but scenery such as this in the Trossachs has witnessed bloody struggles during the shaping of the Scottish state

party. Though she never managed to achieve toleration for the Catholic faith her first years were surprisingly successful. Problems only came to a head with her marriage, in 1565, to her worthless cousin Henry Lord Darnley, who aspired to personal rule. His failed intrigues, shifting allegiances and betrayals soon alienated him from potential supporters but his murder in 1567, followed by the indecently hasty marriage between Queen Mary and the Earl of Bothwell, appalled the nation. By the end of the year Mary had been forced to abdicate in favour of her infant son and Moray, her sinister half-brother, was appointed regent. A failed uprising the next year saw her flee south to England, where her cousin Elizabeth I of England kept her captive for 20 years before ordering her execution.

James VI and the Later Stuarts

It was Mary's wily, intelligent but unprepossessing son, James VI, who eventually enforced peace on his unruly land. He was an exceptional monarch who managed to establish a personal rule by balancing the power of the feuding nobles, increasing the respect for law, quietening the divisions caused by ambitious theologians and developing an efficient administration run by dependable lowland lairds. He even managed to graft together the antagonistic parties of Protestantism to form a broad church that had both bishops and presbyterian councils. This was achieved by a studiously pacific foreign policy, mixed with clemency and patience. It was Scotland's misfortune when he took the road south to inherit the richer crown of England in 1603.

James's descendants lost touch with the spirit of their northern kingdom (and soon after with their southern) so that throughout the 17th century both England and Scotland were riven by a succession of interrelated civil wars. The factions had a fluidity which allowed key characters like the Marquess of Montrose and General David Leslie to cross sides, but were divided on religious grounds, between the Presbyterian Covenanters and the Royalist Episcopalians. The former were the supporters of a church of simple puritanical dignity governed by its elected ministers and elders with support concentrated in the lowlands and southwest. They were ranged against those who wished for a ritualistic church governed by bishops appointed by the king whose core supporters were located in the central Highlands and northeast. It was a bloody and even match until James VII (known in England as James II) drifted into open Catholicism. The Glorious Revolution of 1688 allowed for the victory of the Covenanters, and the Church of Scotland remains a strongly presbyterian institution to this day. Jacobitism, the party that supported the Catholic Stuart monarchs in exile, was thereafter almost exclusively a Highland or Irish affair. In the Lowlands it became little more than a covert after-dinner toast to the king across the water.

BACKGROUND

Late 17th-century glass in Provand's Lordship, Glasgow's oldest house, and closely connected to the Stewart dynasty. James II, James IV and Mary Queen of Scots are all known to have stayed here

Union with England

The Treaty of Union with England in 1707 was partly a celebration of this mutual Protestant victory, but was also brought about by a nationwide bribe. The whole of lowland Scotland's moneyed class, from dukes to village shopkeepers, had heavily invested in the Darien Venture, which was to establish a trading colony in Panama. It was a good idea, but the venture went bankrupt. At this critical psychological moment of national ruin, the English generously offered to cover all losses in exchange for union, which included the worldwide protection services of the Royal Navy and a fair share in the expanding opportunities of their mushrooming empire. In return the Scots accepted the right of the Hanoverian family to succeed to the crown.

Traditional Highland Society

Since the defeat of the Norse in the 13th century the Highlands had seen little change. The highlands and islands were riven into small communities by the dramatic landscape of mountains and sea lochs. It was primarily a cattle breeding society that traded its pastoral products for the grain grown in the lowlands. The cattle, sheep, goats and chickens were highly mobile and every community required a strongly motivated fighting force to protect its wealth from 'lifting'. This was the economic basis of the closely knit and intensely martial Highland clans.

Whatever the actual genetic realities or division of wealth, the clans stressed their unity by claiming descent from a common heroic ancestor. It was a feudal society in which great chiefs granted out land to sub-chieftains who in turn farmed out tacks of land to their cousins, known as tacksmen, who controlled individual glens. Brotherly loyalty within the clan was stressed by the practice of fostering the children of chiefly families in the houses of tenants and by a reciprocal care of the old or destitute by the chief in his hall. The clan chief was a petty sovereign whose status was reflected in his head of cattle and the number of his warrior tenants who dwelt near by in smoke-filled, turf-roofed round huts.

Lowlands against Highlands

Southern Scotland contributed practically everything of material value to the Scottish state and, with the odd exception like Iona, a visitor will find that all the ancient towns, abbeys and ports are situated in the Lowlands.

Bloody encounter during the Jacobite rebellion

The Scottish crown realised it was hopeless to attempt to tax the Highlanders but that the area could be ruled from Edinburgh, by a careful manipulation of the enduring clan rivalries coupled with judicious rewards to the great chiefs. The Highlands brought very limited rewards back to central government but provided a vital resource in times of danger. The mountain valleys could be relied on to produce hardened troops for any military adventure that offered loot, and also to provide an invulnerable refuge against any temporary English occupation of the Lowlands.

This shifting balance of advantage, between the importance of the Highlands in war and the Lowlands in peace, continued throughout Scottish history but changed dramatically at the end of the 17th century. The victory of the Presbyterian party with the accession of William and Mary in 1689 settled over a hundred years of civil strife between the religious factions which had stressed the Highlands' traditional military role within the nation. Worse was to follow, for in 1707 the Treaty of Union between England and Scotland ended the Highlands' old role as a national refuge. The Highland-based Jacobite rebellions in 1715 and 1719 were part of a long history of dissidence but what was new was the Lowland response. General Wade was commissioned to build and design a string of strategic forts and fortified barracks linked by roads and elegant bridges for the military occupation of the Highlands.

1745: The Year of the Prince

The Highland attempt to take the British throne in 1745, led by Bonnie Prince Charlie, has an epic, almost fabulous quality, particularly when viewed from our comparatively colourless times. The year began in April with the landing of the handsome young prince on the coral sands of a West Highland beach. He raised his

standard at Glenfinnan and recruited some of the more martial clans to his cause, winning a succession of impulsive military victories over larger, better-armed government forces. These early successes grew into a triumphant procession delayed only by a series of balls, fêtes and light-hearted affairs before the prince led his Highland army south. The English failed to rally to his cause and he turned back at Derby to be tailed by government forces until forced to give battle at Culloden Moor. The prince's army was destroyed by the superior fire power of its opponents and the Jacobite captives and wounded were treated as traitors and killed without mercy. The Highland people, despite promises of the most enormous reward and threats of dire punishments, sheltered the young prince from an enormous five-month-long manhunt. As the hunt intensified he was whisked away from danger by the heroism of a young girl, the lovely Flora Macdonald, who organised his escape into exile.

Viewed from the longer perspective of Scottish history this looks like an all too familiar refrain – military adventurism threatening the precarious fruits of peace. Most of the clans at the core of the 1745 rebellion were feared in Scotland for their habitual lawlessness, cattle raiding and bullying bellicosity, and the whole adventure could be seen as a cynical spilling of Scottish blood to gain the throne of England by a dynasty that had proved itself totally out of sympathy with its nation.

The Taming of the Highlands

The Hanoverian victory at Culloden Moor was succeeded by a vicious cycle of manhunts, land confiscations and law reform in order to destroy the military basis of Highland society. The powers of the clan chiefs, Highland dress, pipes and weapons were proscribed and a series of ruthless judicial commissions brought the horrid evidence of the gallows to every glen.

Within a few years the Highlands were at peace and money rents began to replace feudal tenures. For a few decades some aspects of life seemed brighter: the potato

Memorial on the site of the Battle of Culloden. During the 40-minute battle 1,200 Scots died; thousands more were killed in the indiscriminate slaughter that followed in the Highlands

provided a new cheap staple crop for the poor, corn prices stayed down and livestock prices soared. The Highlands were virgin territory to capitalists who set up iron foundries and built fishing harbours and woollen mills, partly financed from the profits made by gathering chemical-rich seaweeds. The population doubled within a few decades but the plots of farming land became ever more dangerously small.

The end of the Napoleonic wars brought a violent depression with the total collapse of fish, cattle and kelp prices and the near extinction of rural industries. Only sheep brought in a handsome profit, but sheep farming was incompatible with the thousands of tenants packed into the glens and coastal strips. A few of the Highland landlords, remembering the long traditions of paternalistic care, preferred poverty to the ordering of evictions to make sheep paddocks. Others were forced into the repulsive action by their trustees or bankruptcy courts but many embraced the new policy as the necessary price for self-improvement. Ruined villages can be seen all over the Highlands and the evidence of forced evictions, ordered by the very leaders to whom the people looked for protection, remains like a vivid scar across the landscape. The people were moved south to fill the slums of the industrial cities or packed off in emigrant ships bound for Canada, Australia, New Zealand and the United States.

Traditions kept alive at Blair Castle, with the private army of the Duke of Atholl, the Atholl Highlanders, on parade

The Genius of North Britain, 1760–1860
The consequences for the Lowlands following the final defeat of Jacobitism were altogether more favourable. The energy and achievement that filled the hundred years between 1760 and 1860 is quite astounding. Edinburgh flourished as a city of letters, scientific investigation and medical innovation, seconded by Glasgow which, while not without its theoreticians, tended to attract a more pragmatic turn of mind. Simpson's use of chloroform and Lister's use of antiseptic spearheaded modern surgery. In letters Robert Burns (1759–96), James Hogg, the 'Ettrick shepherd' (1770–1835), James Macpherson of Ossian fame and Sir Walter Scott (1771–1832) had a truly international impact. They were matched by the economics of Adam Smith, the philosophy of Hume and Reid, the physics of Lord Kelvin and the engineering feats of James Watt, Robert Stevenson, Henry Bell and Thomas Telford. The Adam family (William, the father of Robert and three architect brothers) transformed the noble seats of the Lowlands and the streets of Edinburgh into a harmonious classical vision worthy of this period.

The Industrial Revolution
Alongside these intellectual achievements was the amazing transformation of a poor agricultural nation on the outer reaches of European civilisation into the hothouse of the industrial revolution. The merchants of Glasgow were quick to profit from the trans-Atlantic trade with America in the early 18th century. Some of the enormous profits from the slave, sugar, rum, tobacco and cotton trades were ploughed into new machinery and manufacturing techniques. Textiles, iron, chemical, coal, steel, engineering and shipbuilding industries were developed which made the Clyde one of the world's great workshops. Enormous fortunes were made among scenes of appalling urban squalor. It was only during the decline of this energy and industry in the mid-20th century that the rewards began to be shared out more equitably. The discovery of North Sea oil in the early 1960s has helped soften the declining importance of heavy industry.

What to See

The Essential rating system:

✓	'top ten'

♦♦♦   do not miss
♦♦   see if you can
♦   worth seeing if you
      have time

WHAT TO SEE

For the purpose of this guide, Scotland has been divided into eight distinctive regions. The heart of the land is the Forth-Clyde valley which provides Scotland with the bulk of its population and economic strength. The two great rival cities of Edinburgh (pages 21–33) and Glasgow (pages 42–52) are here, and each offers a different facet of the national identity. Try to see both.

To the south rise the Southern Uplands, a wide band of low mountains that stretch across Scotland from coast to coast. The western part is Dumfries and Galloway, the east is known as the Borders (pages 34–41). The area to the north of Edinburgh and Glasgow – Perth, Angus and Fife (pages 61–9) – is now principally agricultural, though it served as the political heart of medieval Scotland. Moving north into the central Highlands, you encounter the grandeur of the Grampians, while around this moorland wilderness stretches the fertile northeast coast, administered by the provincial capitals of Aberdeen and Inverness (pages 70–6). Caithness and Sutherland, north of Inverness, are covered in the chapter on the Far North (pages 85–92), together with the Orkneys and Shetlands.

The west coast has been divided into two chapters: Argyll with Lochaber and the Inner Hebrides (pages 53–60) and Wester Ross with Skye and the Outer Hebrides (pages 77–85). Here the ever-changing combination of mountains, sea, inland lochs, moor and coastal pastures is on an epic scale of beauty and magnificence.

Edinburgh Festival fever

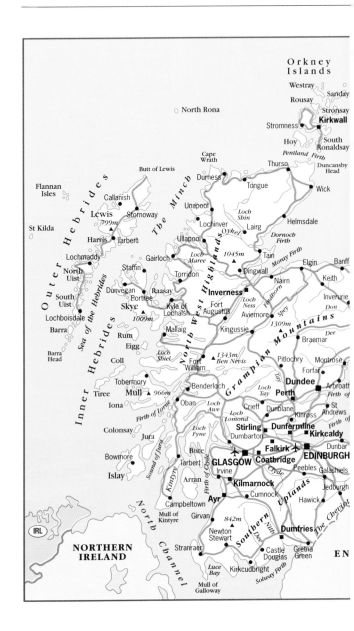

SCOTLAND MAP

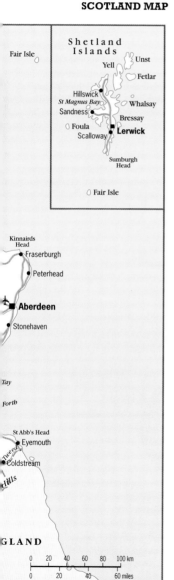

EDINBURGH

Scotland's capital is a city with plenty of open spaces, fine buildings, museums and handsome streets, all clinging to a series of volcanic hills. It is these remnants of ancient volcanoes that provide the astonishing range of street depths, sudden twisting descents, slow stairway climbs and a bewitching variety of changing views.

Edinburgh is an easy city to understand on first acquaintance, though like every great town it has social currents and layers of life and attitudes that can take years to unravel. On the one hand you have the perfectly preserved Georgian New Town, all elegant well-ordered streets, graceful and civilised. On the other you have the Old Town, dark, multi-levelled and dominated by the Castle on its granite heights.

Edinburgh's growth

The Old Town grew over many centuries from the early single road, now the Royal Mile, which ran down the narrow ridge linking the fort on the hill to the Abbey of Holyrood. A close intimacy of all the classes prevailed for many centuries and, though the crowding intensified and the wealth of merchants and aristocrats grew, little attempt was made to expand. It was not until the mid-18th century that prosperous merchants and burghers conceived the notion of building an entirely new city on the gentle land sloping towards the Firth of Forth.

Work commenced immediately and took just one generation to complete. The New Town has always been subject to effective planning controls, and it remains largely as it was intended, with the exception of the modern shop-fronts found on Princes Street.

Of all the institutions of state normally held in a capital Edinburgh keeps only law, finance, education and church. One of the most important cities of Europe during the Age of Enlightenment, and a leading force in the medical and technological inventions of the 19th century, Edinburgh no longer seems to strive to be in the forefront of modernity. Only every August does the city enter the international stage with the world's liveliest arts festival. Otherwise, the usual atmosphere is one of quiet civic pride.

Whatever your viewpoint, the castle is unassailable

◆
CALTON HILL

On this dark, chilly hill to the east of the New Town is the National Monument, honouring the Scots who died in the wars against Napoleon. Started in 1822 as a copy of the Parthenon in Athens, it was abandoned when the money ran out midway through construction. But what had been built looked so dramatic few felt completion would improve it. From the top of the nearby Nelson Monument (shaped like an upturned telescope) you can look down on both Old and New Towns. *Open*: daily.
Closed: Sunday from October to March.

◆◆
CHARLOTTE SQUARE
New Town

In 1792 Robert Adam was employed to build that epitome of the New Town, the handsome Charlotte Square. At number 7 the National Trust for Scotland

has restored the three principal floors of the house into a typical Georgian home; you can gain from it a very good feeling for the civilised style of life that still prevails today throughout the New Town.
Open: daily, Easter to 31 October.
Closed: Sunday mornings.

EDINBURGH CASTLE
summit of Old Town
You can see the castle almost everywhere you go in the city, though its character changes beguilingly from the different points of the compass. The **esplanade**, the first section you come to, was for centuries the scene of executions and mutilations and is the setting for the immensely popular Military Tattoo. The guns formerly mounted in the Castle's Half Moon Battery dominated any approach across the esplanade. Cross the drawbridge past the gaze of the bronze statues of Wallace and Bruce, and signs will point you to the various monuments.
Especially worthy of attention is the tiny **St Margaret's Chapel**, the oldest building in Edinburgh. Measuring only 17 by 11 feet (5 by 3.5m) inside, this early Norman chapel feels like the hidden heart of the city. The strength of feeling expressed in the **Scottish War Memorial** (1927) demonstrates the powerful and deep association between the national psyche and the Scottish soldier. The gracious interior houses a handsome array of regimental memorials.
The Royal Apartments include the little room where James VI of

> **The Edinburgh Festival**
> For three weeks from mid-August Edinburgh changes beyond all recognition. The festival attracts actors, dancers, musicians, film-makers, television producers, book publishers, writers and poets, circus entertainers, mime artists and good-time boys and girls from all over the world. The atmosphere is exhilarating. Everywhere you look some performance is in progress and another is about to begin.
> The official festival is composed of grand works of classical and modern music, opera, theatre and dance, with prestigious international companies and top soloists and conductors. But much of the excitement is generated by the Fringe festival, with members of the festival crowd clocking up five or six shows a day. Meanwhile, on the castle esplanade the military tattoo nightly draws the biggest crowds of any event in the entire nation.
> See also page 108.

Scotland, the first Stuart king of England, was born to Mary Queen of Scots. The Scottish regalia, which includes the crown, sceptre and ceremonial sword, forms the centrepiece of a major exhibition. The double golden circlet is the oldest part of the crown and probably rested on the brow of Robert the Bruce. **Mons Meg**, on display here, is a huge gun forged in the 15th century. Another feature of Edinburgh life is the **One O'Clock Gun**, a more modern weapon fired at that time each day from the Castle ramparts.
Open: daily.

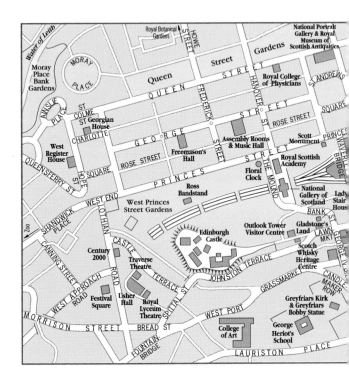

◆◆
GREYFRIARS KIRK
Old Town
It was in the churchyard here that the National Covenant, underlining the principles of the Reformation, was signed (in blood by some) in 1638. Near by in Candlemaker Row is the bronze fountain and statue to Greyfriars Bobby, the Skye terrier who kept vigil at the grave of his dead master for 14 years from 1858. His collar can be seen in the **Museum of Local History**, Huntly House, Canongate.

◆◆◆
HOLYROOD
Old Town
The Palace of Holyroodhouse is the Queen's official Scottish home. She is often in residence in June and early July, when the state apartments are closed (also usually closed for two weeks in May). The earliest fragments of the palace date from around 1530 but most of the house, including the state apartments, was built after the

Holyroodhouse (left) and Arthur's Seat

EDINBURGH CITY MAP

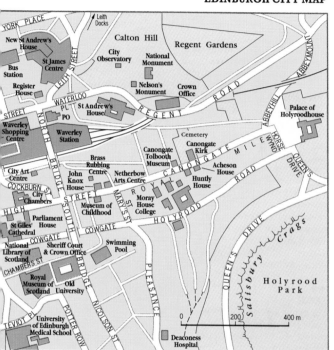

Restoration, on commission from Charles II. In the picture gallery are 111 portraits of Scottish monarchs. The atmosphere changes dramatically as you enter the **Historic Apartments** in which Mary Queen of Scots lived during an eventful six years from 1561. It is here, for example, that Mary saw David Rizzio (her 'favourite') stabbed to death. Near the palace are the ruins of Holyrood Abbey which became the Chapel Royal once the palace had been built. The extensive grounds take in the great volcanic hill **Arthur's Seat**, that overlooks all Edinburgh. It takes between half and three-quarters of an hour to climb to the summit for the best view.
Open: daily.
Closed: mid-May, late June and early July for State visits.

LEITH
For centuries Leith Docks were part of the city's lifeline. In recent years they have become a major bulk grain handler and the elevators now rise above the skyline to dominate the town. Many of Leith's buildings are identical in design to those in the centre of the city, but considerably smaller. Although Leith has become a fashionable residential area, with bright pubs and restaurants, it still seems a doughtier, less worldly place than the city up the hill. There are old buildings to visit, among them **Lamb's House** in Burgess Street, a merchant's home from the early 17th century, and **St Mary's Church**, Kirkgate, of which parts date from the 15th century.

MODERN ART GALLERY
Belford Road
Though only opened in 1984, this absorbing collection contains excellent examples of German Expressionism, Surrealism and French art, as well as works by the great British 20th-century names.
Open: daily.

###
NATIONAL GALLERY OF SCOTLAND
The Mound
A neo-classical building houses the national collection. Since its inception in the 1850s, it has become one of the great collections of Europe. Painters represented here are a roll-call of European art: Raphael, Filippino Lippi, Titian, Tintoretto, Rembrandt, Poussin, Courbet, Gauguin, Monet, Cézanne…
There are portraits by Britain's greatest portrait painters (Gainsborough, Hogarth, Reynolds) and important collections of prints, drawings and watercolours. Scotland is, of course, well represented, by such as Allan Ramsay, Alexander Nasmyth and, most charmingly, Sir Henry Raeburn with *The Reverend Robert Walker Skating on Duddingston Loch*.
Open: daily.
Closed: Sunday morning.

###
PRINCES STREET
New Town
In its heyday Princes Street could boast of being the finest shopping street in Europe; now

*In the beautifully refurbished
National Gallery*

it comprises mostly outlets of
familiar chain retailers.
The most striking landmark on
Princes Street itself is the **Scott
Monument** (closed Sundays),
known from biscuit tins the
world over. Nearly 300 steps
take you near the apex of the
200-foot (60m) gothic spire.
Princes Street Gardens,
which run almost the entire
length of the street, boast the
world's oldest floral clock. At
the base of the castle rock you
will find the **American
Memorial to Scottish Soldiers**,
regarded by many as the most
beautiful war memorial in
Europe.

QUEEN STREET MUSEUMS
Queen Street, New Town
In an orange Italianate building
are two first-rate museums: the
Scottish National Portrait Gallery
and the Museum of Antiquities.
Scottish portraiture has been of
a very high quality, and there is
hardly a bad picture in the
Portrait Gallery, and there are
plenty of famous subjects to
spot: Burns, John Knox, Scott,
Darnley, Mary Queen of Scots
and the great philosopher
David Hume in a particularly

fine portrait by Allan Ramsay.
The **Museum of Antiquities**
covers the culture and history
of man in Scotland, including
major prehistoric, Viking and
Roman collections. For the time
being, however, only one floor
is open, since the museum is
scheduled to move to the new
Museum of Scotland building
currently being built beside the
Royal Museum (see page 30).
Open: daily.
Closed: Sunday morning.

◆
ROSE STREET
New Town
Everyone who knew Bohemian
Rose Street 40 years ago

bewails its commercialisation
and the loss of so intimate a
community of poets, radicals,
artists, musicians and other
heroes. But as a stranger, you
can happily enjoy this 'market
of pubs', sampling the delights
of each one and comparing
them with as much
discrimination as you would
give a fine malt.

◆
ROYAL BOTANIC GARDENS
off Inverleith Row
A welcome break from the
city's bustle, these lie half way
between the city and the Firth of
Forth, directly north of the New
Town. The 65-acre (26ha) site

The Scott (left) and Nelson (right) monuments both afford views of the city and the Firth of Forth

amateur seeker of beauty and seclusion. There are fine modern and Victorian plant houses, and outstanding rhododendrons.
Near by at 8 Howard Place is the birthplace of Robert Louis Stevenson (private).
Gardens open: daily.

◆◆◆
THE ROYAL MILE
Old Town
This walk follows Edinburgh's main thoroughfare from the Castle to the Abbey. A ceremonial way, the landmarks along the Royal Mile take in much of Edinburgh's history. Dark courts, alleys, cobbled streets and steps spin off it at unexpected angles. The road has differently named sections: Castle Hill, Lawnmarket, High Street and Canongate. The **Camera Obscura** (*open:* daily) is near the castle in the Outlook Tower. Of all Edinburgh's fine views, none is better than this reflected one. **Gladstone's Land** in the Lawnmarket (*open:* daily, April to October except Sunday mornings) is the National Trust for Scotland's re-creation of 17th-century domestic life in an Old Town six-storey tenement. **St Giles' Cathedral** was actually a cathedral only in the 17th century and is correctly the High Kirk of Edinburgh. One of the highlights is the Thistle Chapel (1910) draped with the heraldic banners of the Knights of the Thistle.
Canongate was long Edinburgh's most aristocratic quarter, until its glory began to fade with the removal of the

has been in continuous cultivation for 170 years and is as likely to be enjoyed by the expert horticulturalist as by the

---

Dr Jekyll and Mr Hyde
One (or two) of R L Stevenson's most famous characters, Dr Jekyll/Mr Hyde, was based on a real-life Edinburgh character. Deacon Brodie was a master joiner by day and a murderous gangleader by night. When his crimes were discovered he escaped to Holland but was brought back and hanged.

---

court to London in the 17th century. **John Knox House** (closed Sundays), though probably never inhabited by the fiery preacher, is well worth a visit, as is 16th-century **Huntly House** (open: Monday to Saturday), with an excellent and fascinating museum of the history of Edinburgh.

◆◆
ROYAL MUSEUM OF SCOTLAND
Chambers Street, Old Town
This handsome building contains decorative art and archaeology galleries housing local and international exhibits; a natural history section featuring an excellent exhibition on vertebrate evolution; a geology department; and, particularly appealing for children, technological galleries with dozens of superb working models.
Open: daily.
Closed: Sunday morning.

◆
THE (EDINBURGH) ZOO
Corstorphine Road
This large pleasant zoo, about 4 miles (6.5km) to the west of the city centre on the A8, houses many species in spacious, well-tended conditions, including native Scottish species rarely seen in the wild, such as wildcats and pine martens. The world's largest penguin enclosure is here, with three different species taking part in the traditional 'Penguin Parade'.
Open: daily.

NEAR BY
(See map on pages 36–7)

◆◆
BASS ROCK AND TANTALLON CASTLE
25 miles (40km) east of Edinburgh
One and a half miles (2.4km) out to sea the massive Bass Rock rises 313 feet (95m) above the waves. It hosts one of the most important nesting colonies of sea birds in the British Isles. The island of Bass Rock is not open to the public but a boat from North Berwick takes birdwatchers around its coast to see puffins, terns and, especially, gannets (also see Peace and Quiet, page 94). On a rocky mainland promontory overlooking the Bass Rock stand the ruined remains of one of Scotland's most awesome castles, Tantallon, defended by solid rock and its equally solid curtain wall (open: daily; closed: October to March Thursday afternoon and Friday).

The Forth railway bridge

♦♦
DALMENY AND HOPETOUN

Four miles (6km) east of the Forth bridges is Dalmeny House (*open*: July to September Sunday, Monday and Tuesday afternoons). Owned by the Rosebery family, it contains the Rothschild Mentmore collection of 17th-century French furniture, tapestry and Sèvres porcelain.

Four miles (6km) to the west of the bridges is Hopetoun House (*open*: daily, in summer), the magnificent home of the Marquess of Linlithgow, built by Sir William Bruce with additions by William Adam and his sons. Inside are splendid paintings, tapestries and furniture.

♦
FORTH BRIDGES

The Forth rail bridge celebrated its 100th birthday in 1990 and for many years was the world's longest bridge. It was the first such structure to be made of cast steel, and remains a much admired engineering feat. To the west is the magnificent suspension road bridge built in 1964, considerably longer and lighter than the rail bridge.

♦♦
LINLITHGOW PALACE

about 15 miles (24km) west of Edinburgh

The great, ruined Stuart Renaissance palace of Linlithgow, birthplace of James V and his daughter Mary Queen of Scots, stands above the long high street of the town and overlooks the small loch. The palace can easily be taken in *en route* from Edinburgh to Glasgow. An impressive octagonal fountain stands in the courtyard, on one side of which is the vast Great Hall. You can picnic on the stretch of turf that surrounds the outer walls of the palace. *Open*: daily.

Penguin march past at the zoo

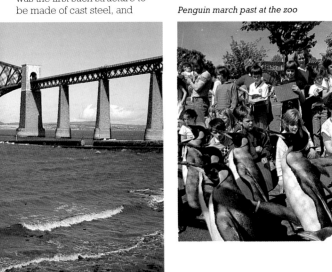

*Rosslyn Chapel, a fitting burial
vault for hereditary Grand Master
Masons*

♦♦♦
ROSSLYN CHAPEL ✓

On the road south out of
Edinburgh, towards Penicuik
(A702) you will see signs to
Roslin (*sic*) as you enter the
Pentland Hills. You will first see
the ruins of Rosslyn Castle (not
open) where the mighty Earl of
Orkney lived in the 15th
century. Some 220 yards
(200m) away stands the
beautiful Rosslyn Chapel,
founded by Sir William St Clair
and a showcase of exquisite
15th-century craftsmanship. The
short pillars dividing the central
aisle bear lovely carvings,
among them an angel playing
the bagpipes. The Prentice Pillar
is said to have been carved by
an apprentice, and that he was
struck dead by his jealous
master when the master saw the
quality of the workmanship. Ten
of the St Clair barons are buried
here in their armour.
Open: daily.

PRACTICALITIES
The telephone area code for
Edinburgh is 0131.

Accommodation
The **Caledonian** ('the Cally'
tel: 459 9988), on the site of an
old railway station, has some of
the style and grandeur offered
the Victorian tourist. The other
great station hotel, recently
renamed the **Balmoral** (tel: 556
2414), but still known in the city
as the North British, stands
above Waverley Station.
Another first-rate, central hotel
is the **Carlton Highland** (tel:
556 7277), at North Bridge.
Less pricey are the **Mount
Royal** (tel: 225 7161) or the
Old Waverley (tel: 556 4648)
which are pleasant and central.
Of the chain hotels, both the
Capital Moat House (tel: 535
9988) and the **Forte Posthouse**
(tel: 334 0390) offer excellent
accommodation and service in
central locations. Two modest
but good hotels are the
Rothesay (tel: 225 4125) and
Suffolk Hall (tel: 668 4333).
There are also many guest
houses and private B & Bs,
particularly in the Newington
Area south of the University
(see also page107).

Eating Out
If you're looking for a meal, the
best area to try is probably
north of Princes Street.
Cousteau's, 47 Hill Street Lane
North (tel: 226 3355), is a
quality (though expensive)
seafood restaurant.
Bar Napoli, 75 Hanover Street
(tel: 225 2600), is one of the
breeziest of the many
entertaining Italian restaurants

backed up by the **Tinelli**, a North Italian *ristorante* found at 139 Easter Road (tel: 652 1932). **Kalpna**, 2 St Patrick Street (tel: 667 9890). Excellent and cheap no-smoking restaurant serving Gujerati vegetarian food. **Martins**, 70 Rose Street (tel: 225 3106). Martin and Gay Irons make skilful use of their fresh supplies of organically grown vegetables and herbs to serve meals such as fresh sorrel soup followed by duck breast with lentils and bramble sauce. **The Vintners Room** (tel: 554 6767) offers excellent food in a former Georgian warehouse, or try **Pierre Victoire** at 38 Grassmarket and 10 Victoria Street (tel: 225 1721), or its Italian sister, **Pepe Vittorio** in Victoria Street (tel: 226 7267). For the best of modern Scottish cuisine, book a table at **The Atrium** (tel: 228 8882).

Nightlife

The changing venues, clubs and bars of the music and disco scene are monitored by the fortnightly *The List* magazine. The leading venues include **Honeycomb**, 36–8 Blair Street,

Century 2000 at 31 Lothian Road, and the **Rocking Horse** at Cowgate for dancing. Listen to rock and blues at **Las Rock Café**, West Port and the **Venue**, Calton Road, with Jazz at **Fat Sam's** in Fountainbridge. For those with more sober tastes, Edinburgh can offer theatre – the Victorian **Royal Lyceum** has a resident company and the **Traverse Theatre** in Cambridge Street is known for its innovative work – concerts (the **Usher Hall** and **Queens Hall** are the main venues) and six multiscreen cinemas as well as the Filmhouse. During the Festival scores of venues throughout the city feature the widest variety of performances. Scottish evenings are also very popular with visitors (usually a show and dinner). Ask the Tourist Office for details.

Shopping

Princes Street is the main shopping centre of the city. **Valvona and Crolla**, at the top of Leith Walk, an Italian-run grocery shop, is one of the best food shops in the country.

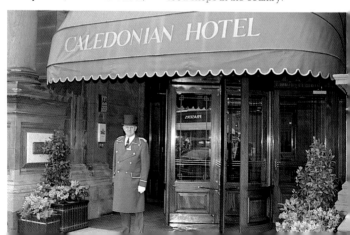

THE BORDER COUNTRY

Scotland's best-known writers, Robert Burns and Sir Walter Scott, have familiarised the world with this area's language, people and landscapes. John Buchan in this century exemplified the local character to millions of readers: self-reliance and doughty self-confidence.

Few regions of Europe have witnessed such intense strife over so many centuries as the Borders. The skirmishes of Roman times were succeeded by Irish, German, then Norse raider-settlers who in turn gave way to ferocious local power struggles. In the medieval period this evolved into murderous national struggles against the English kings. The tragedies of those times are remembered everywhere, signalled by the frequent pele towers.

No other part of Scotland boasts such a wealth of fine houses or imposing castles; the private collections of painting, furniture and antiquities rival those in the great cities. At the same time, the quality of scenery for walking or riding, the excellence of the golf, fishing and swimming make this an excellent area for outdoor pursuits.

The area has been divided into two, roughly on the line of the A74 motorway. The east (the modern Borders Region, composed of the four old counties of Peebles, Selkirk, Berwick and Roxburgh) has the glorious Tweed, abounding in salmon and trout, the great woollen mills of the 19th century, the wooded lowlands and mild heathered hills and many noble houses and castles. The west, consisting of Dumfries, Galloway and Ayrshire, is more subdued, the hills gloomier and wilder. This is the country of Burns, Wallace, Robert the Bruce and the stern Covenanters of the 17th-century Reformation.

The dining room at Abbotsford House, where Sir Walter Scott died in 1832

THE BORDERS

◆◆◆
ABBOTSFORD HOUSE ✓

between Galashiels and Melrose
Walter Scott's home, still lived in by his descendants, is the romantic turreted mansion he built on the banks of the Tweed. It contains Scott's extraordinary collection of armour, antiquities and various Scottish curiosities: a lock of Bonnie Prince Charlie's hair; Queen Mary's seal; the massive keys from the old Edinburgh tolbooth; the armour and two-handed sword of the giant Sir John Cheney. Testimonials to Scott's genius from his contemporaries (one suspects they were as prominent in his lifetime as they are today) litter the house. The gardens are less engaging than the house but have a charming tearoom set in a greenhouse designed by Scott.
Open: daily, March to October.
Closed: Sunday mornings.

◆◆
BOWHILL HOUSE
3 miles (5km) west of Selkirk
Set on high ground between the two best-loved tributaries of the Tweed – the Yarrow and the Ettrick – the home of the Scotts of Buccleuch dates mainly from the 19th century. It contains many fine works of art including the last privately-owned Leonardo in Britain. The wooded grounds contain an exciting adventure playground.
Open: house: weekday afternoons in July; grounds: afternoons April to August.

Dryburgh Abbey – final resting place of Walter Scott and Earl Haig

◆◆◆
DRYBURGH ABBEY ✓

outside Newtown St Boswells
In a tranquil and lovely situation on the Tweed, this is the most rewarding to visit of the Borders abbeys (see **Jedburgh**). Large sections are well preserved, especially the evocative cloisters. A contemplative walk here makes all the difference to your enjoyment of the peace of Scotland's serenest ruin. Leave your car in the village and cross the river by the footbridge (you can always reward yourself later at the hotel that stands beside the ruins).
Open: daily.

◆◆
FLOORS CASTLE
northwestern edge of Kelso
The castellated core of Floors, Scotland's largest inhabited castle, was designed by William Adam, with wings

THE BORDER COUNTRY

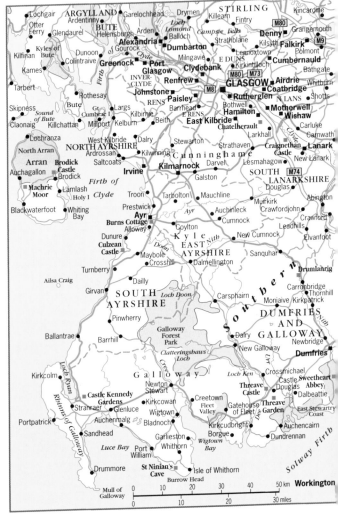

added by W H Playfair in the
19th century. The result is one
of the stateliest exteriors of all

the Border palaces, fitting
happily into a park overlooking
the River Tweed and with a

BORDER COUNTRY MAP

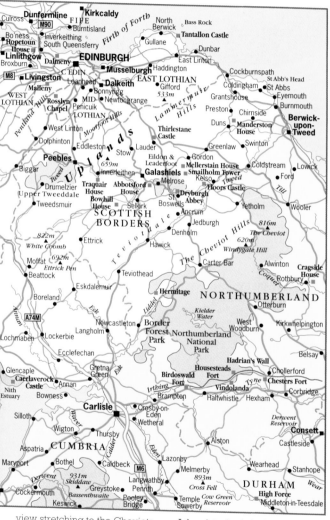

view stretching to the Cheviots. The ducal Roxburghe family own the castle. The only original Adam interior is in the hall, but there are many treasures elsewhere in the house: an

The harbour at St Abbs

outstanding collection of early Flemish and Gobelin tapestries, French furniture from the 17th and 18th centuries and the 19th-century Gothick bird room.
Open: April to September (not Fridays and Saturdays).

◆◆
JEDBURGH ABBEY
There is no more striking testament to border strife than the ruins of the four great abbeys, founded in the 12th century, by King David I (the others were Dryburgh, Kelso and Melrose). Jedburgh Abbey was destroyed and rebuilt eight times. Look out in particular for two late Norman doorways and the tracery of the window in the north transept.
Open: daily.

◆
KELSO ABBEY AND TOWN
This ruin is perhaps the least appealing of the four Borders abbeys. It most resembled a fortress; indeed its massive square tower was used as a castle keep by the townspeople

on the day of its eventual destruction.
Kelso itself is the most handsome of all the border towns, with its great square and extensive civic spaces, all set close to the River Tweed.
Open: Abbey: at all reasonable times.

◆◆
MANDERSTON HOUSE
2 miles (3.2km) east of Duns
The perfectly preserved staff quarters are the most fascinating part of this fine Edwardian country house, affording an insight into the life and conditions experienced by the scores of domestics who ran such houses. The stables are an equine palace, with teak stalls and marble mangers. A park of 56 acres (22ha) contains splendid walks through woods, by loch shores or through formal and graceful pleasure gardens.
Open: May to September Thursday and Sunday afternoons.

MELLERSTAIN HOUSE
6 miles (9.5km) northwest of Kelso
This lovely Georgian house was started by William Adam and extended by his son Robert. It is everything one expects of an Adam house: stately yet comfortable; spacious and light. The rooms, though lived in for 250 years, retain a new-minted freshness with their decorated ceilings in pastel Adam colours. Do not miss the portrait of Bonnie Prince Charlie disguised as Flora Macdonald's Irish maid, Betty Burke, displayed in a small museum at the top of the house.
Open: May to September Sunday to Friday.

MELROSE ABBEY
The soft pink ruins of the abbey in the centre of Melrose town represent the high point in the golden age of Scottish ecclesiastical architecture. It is a magical site. The spell book of the 13th-century wizard Michael Scott lies buried in the grounds, as does the heart of Robert the Bruce. In the grounds also is an apple orchard while, just outside, the National Trust for Scotland has established a traditional walled herb garden.
Open: daily.

ST ABBS
5 miles (8km) north of Eyemouth
The fishing village of St Abbs, though well hidden from the coast road, is easy to identify from the sea by its cliff-top church. The harbour makes an attractive start for two walks: one south to the sandy beach in Coldingham Bay, the other north along the cliffs to the 300-foot (100m) St Abb's Head, at the heart of a 200-acre (80ha) bird reserve (see page 101).

TRAQUAIR HOUSE
about 6 miles (9.5km) east of Peebles
Traquair House is possibly Scotland's oldest inhabited house. Very dark and chilly inside – no part more so than the icy state rooms of the 15th century – the mansion yet has a friendly atmosphere, generated by the family that lives there. The Bear Gates were closed in 1776 and will only be opened when a Scottish monarch ascends the throne. In the gardens is a splendid maze and beer is brewed, for sale in the souvenir shop.
Open: daily, May to September.

Common Ridings
Every year, the inhabitants of the principal Borders towns set aside one summer day to ride along their boundaries on horseback, beating the posts to re-assert their ancient rights to the territories delineated. The day of the riding is followed by a general festival lasting a week or a fortnight. Visitors are welcome. The towns involved and the sequence of their festivals are: West Linton (early June), Hawick, Selkirk, Melrose, Peebles, Galashiels, Duns, Jedburgh, Kelso, Lauder and Coldstream.

THE BORDER COUNTRY

AYRSHIRE, DUMFRIES AND GALLOWAY

◆◆
ALLOWAY

Here is the cottage, built by his father's hands, where Robert Burns was born in 1759. Next door is the **Burns Museum**, containing many artefacts and manuscripts relating to the great man. Near by, the popular **Land of Burns** centre uses audiovisual displays to put the poet in the context of 18th-century Ayr society.
Open: daily.
Closed: November to March Sundays.

◆◆
AYR

A cheerful, spacious, town with splendid sandy beaches, Ayr is famous for golf and for Scotland's premier race course, where the Scottish Grand National is run in April. Little remains of historic Ayr other than the 13th-century **Auld Brig** (Old Bridge). In **Mauchline**, a village 10 miles (16km) east of Ayr, is **Poosie Nansie's Tavern**, scene of Burns' poem *The Jolly Beggars.*

◆
CAERLAVEROCK CASTLE

6 miles (9.5km) southeast of Dumfries
The triangular plan, full moat and delightfully peaceful position beside the Solway Firth make this one of the most satisfying castles in the country. Within the outer walls, the interior has a fine Renaissance façade added in the 17th century. Close by is a superb bird reserve of the Wildfowl

Trust (see also page 102).
Open: Castle: daily; reserve: September to April.

◆◆◆
CULZEAN CASTLE AND COUNTRY PARK

12 miles (19km) southwest of Ayr
The ancient seat of the Kennedys, perched on a cliff top, has arguably the finest Adam interior in the country, behind a betowered and battlemented exterior. The celebrated Oval Staircase rises through three tiers of columns to the splendid first-floor Salon. There is a 560-acre (225ha) park with walled summer garden, Italianate terraces, lake and glass houses. South of Culzean is the famous Turnberry golf course on the dunes beside castle ruins and a lighthouse.
Open: daily, April to October.

◆◆◆
DRUMLANRIG

3 miles (5km) north of the village of Thornhill
This enormous pink sandstone palace with its corner towers, the seat of the Duke of Buccleuch, was built in the 17th century for the 1st Duke of Queensberry. It has the region's finest collection of old masters and exquisite 18th-century French furniture.
Open: daily, except Thursday May to August.

◆
KIRKCUDBRIGHT

This pretty town on the River Dee has attracted Scottish artists since the early years of the century. It is a tranquil spot to spend a leisurely day, walking through the streets and along the river bank, looking over the ancient tolbooth or visiting the **Stewartry Museum**.

◆
LARGS
The coastal resort of Largs is linked to Glasgow by rail and comes complete with its own golf course, yacht marina, beaches and a ferry to the Cumbrae Isles. It is famous for **Nardini's**, a Scottish-Italian ice-cream parlour of unaltered 1930s architecture.

◆◆
THREAVE CASTLE AND THREAVE GARDEN
Three miles (5km) west of Castle Douglas, on the A75, are a grim castle and a lovely garden. The castle was built by Archibald the Grim, 3rd Earl of Douglas, who boasted how the 'gallows knob' that sticks out of the castle's front 'never wanted a tassel'. The nearby Threave Garden is where the National Trust for Scotland trains its gardeners. Here is every possible gardening terrain and form, with

Drumlanrig Castle, set among woodland in Nithsdale

rose and heather beds, rockeries, woodland and herbaceous border.
Open: Castle: daily in summer; garden: all year.

ACCOMMODATION AND EATING OUT
Think about staying in Ayr in the west and Peebles or Kelso in the east.
Ayr
The best hotel is the **Caledonian Hotel**, on Dalblair Road (tel: 01292 269331). Near by you can eat at the **Tudor** (tel: 01292 261404) or the **Hunny Pot** (tel: 01292 289236).
Peebles
A country house hotel with a good restaurant is the **Cringletie House Hotel**, Peebles, Lothian (tel: 01721 730233). It is closed from January to March. The **Tontine Hotel** on the High Street (tel: 01721 720892) is open all year round.
Kelso
Three miles (5km) from the town is the **Sunlaws House Hotel** (tel: 01573 450331) with a vast garden and a hearty restaurant. In town the **Ednam House Hotel**, Bridge Street (tel: 01573 224163) is a friendly fishing hotel.

GLASGOW

Approaching Glasgow along the M8, the skyline of chimneys, cranes, factories and tower blocks is strangely beautiful, a vivid symbol of the city's industrial roots. Entering the city centre, you find a different kind of energy and charm, the result of a successful Victorian commerce. Many of Glasgow's fine buildings and collections were left by great merchant dynasties, including the treasures in the Kelvingrove and Hunterian museums and the huge Burrell Collection. Many of the main sights are in west and central Glasgow and can be covered on foot – the neat grid system of streets makes it easy to find your way. For more outlying places, be prepared to use the city's well-developed transport services.

Thinking at the Burrell Collection

Glasgow Yesterday and Today

It was Glasgow's enterprise that lifted Scotland from the outer fringes of European civilisation to centre stage. Here, more than in any other city in Britain, can be seen the processes that forged the industrial revolution. In the 17th century, the city merchants were earning a fortune from the triangular trade of the Atlantic: shipping slaves out to the Americas from West Africa and exporting sugar or rum back to Europe. From 1715 to the 1770s, the focus turned to tobacco, spawning 'Tobacco Lords' who later invested their huge fortunes in new industries: textiles, chemicals, coal mining, iron-manufacture and cotton.

Emphasis later switched to engineering and shipbuilding with many of the world's greatest liners built on the Clyde. In the 19th century Glasgow was the workshop of the British Empire, if not of the world.

The city centre's solid Victorian face is testament to past fortunes, but in the 20th century the infamous tenement housing developments of the Gorbals, cited as the poorest living area in Europe, gave Glasgow an unenviable reputation. The Gorbals tenements were replaced by even more unpopular tower blocks, and the surplus post-war population moved out to satellite New Towns. Today, most of the tower blocks have gone and, though there is still poverty, Glasgow is now celebrated for its busy bars, stylish shops, innovative arts... and the snappiest hairstyles in Europe.

to every kind and period of European art, including Sir William's personal favourites – medieval glass and tapestries. Despite the size of this collection, it avoids any feeling of pressure to 'get round it all'.
Open: daily.

◆◆
GALLERY OF MODERN ART
Queen Street and Royal Exchange Square
Royal Exchange Square is one of the most graceful in the city and a fit setting for this newly opened gallery. The building, dating from the 18th century was once the Royal Exchange and more recently home to the Stirling Library. The collection contains the best of Scottish and international art, sculpture, craft, design and paintings.
Open: daily.

◆◆
GLASGOW ART GALLERY AND MUSEUM
Kelvingrove Park
Since the mid-19th century some of Glasgow's richest industrial giants have bequeathed their collections to the city gallery and museum. Many of the pictures came through the Glasgow art dealer Alexander Reid (who was painted by Van Gogh). The museum spans the ages from neolithic artefacts to Cubist paintings by way of 17th-century Dutch and Flemish works. In the French galleries one can trace the progression from Millet and Daubigny to Monet and Pissarro, extending the artistic journey to Braque, Picasso, Matisse and the Fauvists.
Open: daily.

◆
THE BARRAS
east of High Street
This rabbit warren of streets and stalls is a haven for browsers and has been going since medieval times.
Open: weekends.

◆◆◆
THE BURRELL COLLECTION ✓

Pollok Country Park
Shipowner Sir William Burrell (1861–1958) left his extraordinary art collection to the people of the city of Glasgow, with strict instructions that it should be housed 'in a rural setting far removed from the atmospheric pollution of urban conurbations'.
His wishes have been fulfilled in the glass-walled building opened in 1983 in the grounds of Pollok House. The vast collection ranges from Chinese ceramics and Japanese prints

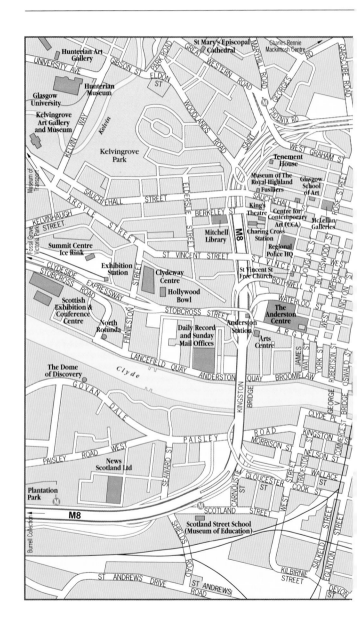

GLASGOW CITY MAP

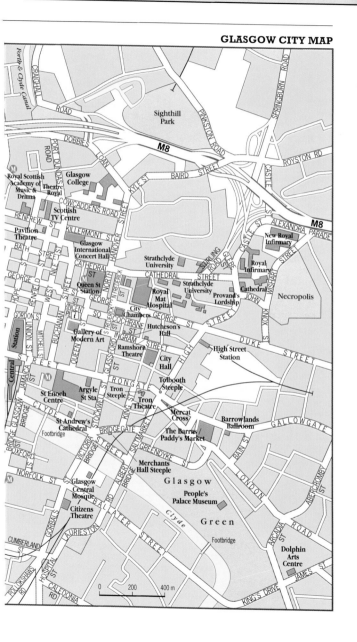

GLASGOW CATHEDRAL

Cathedral Square, Castle Street
Work began on the sombre
Gothic cathedral in the 12th
century, to be completed some
300 years later. The choir and
lower church are 13th century,
a riot of pointed arches, with
highly decorated capitals. In the
lower church is the tomb of
St Mungo and the St Kentigern
Tapestry (1979) which depicts
various scenes from the life of
Glasgow's patron saint (who
goes by both names). From the
northernmost chapel, a door
leads to the upper chapter
room, where students at the
medieval university were given
classes.
Open: daily.

GLASGOW SCHOOL OF ART

Renfrew Street
The school, designed when he
was only 28, is the best
finished example of a Charles
Rennie Mackintosh building.
Completed in 1909, it contains
many of his designs for
furnishings and fixtures, and
also paintings. The massive
windows and suspended
ceiling have made the library
his most admired interior
work.
Open: Monday to Friday in
summer (guided tours).

HUNTERIAN ART GALLERY

*Hillhead Street, off University
Avenue*
The Hunterian gallery, built in
1980, houses Glasgow
University's art collection.

Glasgow's Patron Saint
A Christian cemetery was
established in the 5th century at
Cathures, on the banks of the
Molendinar Burn, by St Ninian
of Whithorn. It was here that
St Mungo came in the next
century to officiate at a burial.
He stayed and built a chapel
called 'Glaschu', meaning
'Dear Green Place', the seed
from which the great city grew.
The Blacader Aisle in the
cathedral is believed to mark
the site of Cathures.

Dr William Hunter bequeathed
the core of the collection to the
University in the 18th century.
It has been much augmented
since and includes outstanding
old masters. It is also
renowned for the most
comprehensive collection
anywhere of the works and
possessions of James McNeill
Whistler (1834–1903) and
Scottish art of the 19th and
20th centuries.
The gallery's tower contains the
Mackintosh Wing where the
Glasgow house, once lived in
and furnished by the great
designer, is cleverly
reproduced. Charles Rennie
Mackintosh had an enormous
influence across Europe and
America, though the surviving
corpus of his work is
comparatively slight, which
makes this reconstruction all
the more valuable. Pieces of
original furniture have been
acquired or copied and placed
in an interior dominated by
clean lines and white painted
woodwork.
Open: Monday to Saturday.

◆
HUNTERIAN MUSEUM
University Avenue (almost opposite the Art Gallery)
The coin and medal display, the richest outside Paris, is the core of this antiquarian collection: Scotland's first coin, not struck until 1136, is here. Evidence from the Roman occupation, Captain Cook's voyages and prehistory are displayed in the main hall, with Scotland's only dinosaur in the upper gallery.
Open: Monday to Saturday.

◆◆
MUSEUM OF TRANSPORT
Kelvin Hall, 1 Bunhouse Road
This gleaming and comprehensive collection of historic transport vehicles includes horse carriages, bicycles, trams, trolleys, trains and cars and is a positive treat for all ages. Do not expect to leave in under twice the time you allowed (more if you are with a child). Outside the main block, look for the collection of scale model ships, many of the full-size versions of which were Clyde-built.
Open: daily.

Mackintosh design at the Hunterian Art Gallery

◆◆
THE NECROPOLIS
east of the Cathedral
The 19th-century Necropolis bravely ran against the grain of Glasgow's long-established sectarian divisions, allowing Protestants, Catholics, Freethinkers and Jews to lie in proximity under Egyptian obelisks, Greek urns, broken Roman columns, gothic pinnacles, baroque portals and idealised statues. Among the avenues are the tombs of the bleach-making Tennants whose company grew into ICI, of Corlinda Lee, Queen of the Gypsies and of William Miller, chiefly famed for originating the Wee Willie Winkie nursery rhyme. Look for the statues of Scotland's most famous explorer David Livingstone and, at the highest point, that great presbyterian preacher, John Knox. From here you get the finest view of the cathedral. There is also a statue of Dutch King William of Orange situated in Cathedral Square.

♦♦
PEOPLE'S PALACE

Glasgow Green
This 19th-century sandstone building is backed by the opulent glass conservatory of the Winter Gardens, furnished with palms, a teahouse and a shop. In the main building is an informal museum of Glasgow life with a strong political element. The slow rise in trade union power is chronicled alongside more famous aspects of the city's history such as James Watt and the invention of the steam engine.
Open: daily.

♦
PROVAND'S LORDSHIP

3 Castle Street
The carefully restored medieval exterior of Provand's Lordship (built for the prebend of Provan, one of the Cathedral canons) stands below the cathedral. The only pre-Reformation house to survive from the old burgh that clustered around the cathedral, castle and Molendinar Burn, it now houses a well-displayed museum of Glasgow's past.
Open: daily.

Founded in 1471, Provand's Lordship is the oldest house in Glasgow

♦♦♦
TENEMENT HOUSE ✓

145 Buccleuch Street
The National Trust for Scotland has preserved this simple city-centre flat, which was once the home of Miss Agnes Toward, just as she left it in 1965. Her collection of old bills, postcards and letters, amassed from 1911, combined with the plain orderliness of her small furnished flat in a shared close, provides insight into the everyday life of the recent past.
Open: afternoons, March to October.

Tenement House keeps domestic memories alive

NEAR BY
See map on page 36.

◆◆
BOTHWELL
8 miles (13km) southeast of Glasgow
Bothwell has a 14th-century church, a monument by its bridge recalling a defeat of the Covenanters and, its main claim to fame, the towers and mighty curtain walls that comprise **Bothwell Castle** (*open*: daily). Set commandingly, high above the River Clyde, the ruins date from the late 13th to 15th centuries. The castle became the preferred headquarters of the English kings, for which reason it was intentionally destroyed in 1337. The Border Douglas Earls later repaired it for their use.

◆◆
CHATELHERAULT
just south of Hamilton
The grand palace of the dukes of Hamilton was demolished in 1927, but visitors can still see the 'Dogg Kennell', a hunting lodge designed by William Adam. Named after the French dukedom held by the Hamiltons, Chatelherault stands on the edge of the Avon gorge. The planting in the walled garden follows the original plan and the plasterwork in the interior has been recreated in its original grandeur. The wooded country park around Chatelherault contains the ruins of royal **Cadzo Castle** and ancient oaks said to have been planted by David I in the early 12th century.
Open: daily.

Bothwell Castle

◆◆
CRAIGNETHAN CASTLE
5 miles (8km) northwest of Lanark
Built between 1530 and 1540 by Sir James Hamilton of Finnart, the castle has a fine example of a caponier – a vaulted gallery constructed in the dry moat. This protected the defenders inside from artillery fire. It is thought to be the earliest example of this defence design in Britain, needed here because, as strong partisans of Mary Queen of Scots, the Hamiltons suffered attacks when she fled to England. In 1665 the Hay family built a new, more comfortable house in the courtyard using stone from the original castle.
Open: March to October.
Closed: Thursday afternoon and Friday.

◆
DUMBARTON ROCK
10 miles (16km) northwest of Glasgow
The twin-peaked volcanic plug of Dumbarton Rock was, with its castle and port, the ancient capital of the Kingdom of Strathclyde. The present castle (*open*: daily) is a series of 18th-century buildings and terraces providing fine views across and up the Clyde towards Glasgow. Dumbarton itself is an industrial town, with only a few reminders of its ancient past.

◆◆
HAMILTON
10 miles (16km southeast of Glasgow)
Known as Cadzo until the 15th century, Hamilton was renamed after the powerful dynasty who established themselves here. Later it became an industrial centre. In what were the Low Parks of the Hamiltons' estate is an impressive, if eccentric sight – the **Hamilton Mausoleum**. Commissioned by Alexander, 10th Duke of Hamilton (known as El Magnifico), it took 15 years to build. It could not be used for its original purpose – as a chapel – because of its astonishing echo; Alexander was buried there in an Egyptian sarcophagus in 1852.
Open: weekends (guided tours).

◆◆
NEW LANARK
outside Lanark, 26 miles (42km) southeast of Glasgow
The 18th-century model mill town of New Lanark has happily been preserved. It has connections with many leaders of the industrial revolution such as the inventor Richard Arkwright, the banker David Dale and the latter's son-in-law Robert Owen (1771–1858), who, through enlightened programmes of education and social care, created a successful industrial community alongside a profitable and efficient cotton mill. The excellent visitor centre (*open*: daily) established in the old cotton mill offers 'The Annie McLeod Experience', a Disneyesque history ride, together with shops and a café-restaurant.

◆
PAISLEY
5 miles (8km) southwest of Glasgow
Paisley's suburbs have merged with those of the big city beside it. The museum in the High Street (*closed*: Sundays and holidays) has a fine local history display, as well as over 700 of the Paisley shawls and plaids for which the town is famous. Don't miss Paisley Abbey, with its towering Gothic nave.

Paisley Shawls
At the end of the 18th century, returning soldiers brought beautiful shawls with intriguing designs back from India. These were soon copied in several places in Britain, but nowhere more successfully than in Paisley where there were well-established thread-making and weaving mills. The 'Paisley pattern' or 'pine' motif – still popular today – actually originated in Kashmir.

PRACTICALITIES
The telephone area code for Glasgow is 0141.

Accommodation
To treat yourself, try **One Devonshire Gardens** (tel: 339 2001). It occupies three adjoining town houses with a lavish but homely Victorian interior, marble bathrooms, a bar, residents' dining room and a separate public restaurant. Also highly recommended is the **Moat House International** (tel: 306 9988). Modern and good are the **Forte Crest** (tel: 248 2656) and the **Glasgow Thistle** (tel: 332 3311). For individual character try the **Devonshire** (tel: 339 7878) or the **Town House** (tel: 332 3320). In the city centre is the **Buchanan Hotel**, 185 Buchanan Street (tel: 332 7284). This friendly hotel with its

Full house at the Kings Theatre, a splendid Edwardian building with a history of first-class productions

Italian restaurant occupies a Victorian building. Cheaper accommodation in the city centre can be found along Renfrew Street, parallel to Sauchiehall Street.

Eating Out
Glasgow is not short of charming cafés and wine bars, often run by Italians, many of whose forebears came to the city as political exiles in the 19th century.
Café Gandolfi, 64 Albion Street (tel: 552 6813). There can be few better ways to start the day than with a steaming cappuccino and hot croissant in this comfortable café.
Sarti's, Wellington Street. A bustling delicatessen with café tables for coffee or meals – try the delicious pasta or *ciabatta* bread rolls stuffed with salami and cheese.
Babbity Bowster Hotel, Blackfriars Street (tel: 552 5055). A combination of wine

St Enoch's shopping centre

bar, café and restaurant.
There are even a few rooms
available upstairs.
Fazzi Café, Cambridge Street.
Italian-style delicatessen with
café attached.
Rogano, 11 Exchange Place,
(tel: 248 4055). Dine in the
spectacular 1930s setting of
Glasgow's most popular fish
restaurant and oyster bar – a
unique experience.
The **Buttery**, 652 Argyle Street
(tel: 221 8188) is a genuine
survival of Victorian Glasgow.

Nightlife
Glasgow has eight permanent
theatres and concert halls,
opera and ballet companies,
two dozen clubs and an equal
number of bars where you
can hear live folk, jazz or
country and western. Coolest
dance venues are The Arches
and Glasgow School of Art,
otherwise buy a copy of the
fortnightly *The List* magazine
for programme details. See
also page 108.

Shopping
Most of the large department
stores are found in Argyle,
Buchanan and Sauchiehall
streets with a selection of
antique shops in West Regent
Street, Great Western and
Byres Roads. **Princes Square**
has up-market shops and the
St Enoch's Centre is housed
beneath the largest glass roof
in Europe and includes a
skating rink. For continental
elegance however, browse the
Italian Centre, off George
Square. The **Edinburgh
Woollen Mill** at 75 St George's
Place and **Pitlochry Knitwear**
at 130 Buchanan Street have a
fine selection of tweeds and
woollens.

ARGYLL, LOCHABER AND THE INNER ISLES

Argyll, 'the coast of the Gaels', is arguably Scotland's most beautiful region. It is divided into a collection of narrow peninsulas by great sea lochs – Long, Fyne, and Etive – and is defined by Glencoe in the north, Loch Lomond in the east and a scattering of western isles that reach towards Ireland. This chapter goes beyond Argyll's historic frontiers to include Fort William and Mallaig.

◆◆
ARRAN

The largest of the Clyde Islands, Arran is hilly in the north, pastoral in the south. The southwest quarter is littered with alluring stone circles for history buffs, while the diverse island wildlife should satisfy the nature lover. **Brodick Castle** (*open*: Easter to October) has been a stronghold of the Earls of Arran since 1503. The lovely grounds contain countless rhododendrons and a pavilion made from tree bark and nuts.

◆
BUTE

Glaswegians still like to cross the narrow Kyles of Bute for a short excursion to the busy resort of Rothesay on the island of Bute. In August, the 11-day Highland Festival draws hordes of visitors. Much of the entertainment is staged within the circular walls of **Rothesay Castle** (*open*: daily; *closed*: October to March Friday). The gothic Mount Stuart is also now open to the public.

◆
CAMPBELTOWN AND MULL OF KINTYRE

Kintyre peninsula
It was from Campbeltown that Flora Macdonald set sail for North Carolina in 1774. **Davaar Island** lies off the entrance to the bay here, accessible across a shingle bank at low tide, otherwise by ferry, for Davaar's Cave containing a strange painting of the Crucifixion by Archibald Mackinnon (1887). The Mull of Kintyre, the rocky tip of the peninsula, was made famous in a song by former Beatle Paul McCartney, who lives here.

◆
FORT WILLIAM

This resort is dominated in all senses by **Ben Nevis**. To get to the top of Britain's highest mountain (4,411 feet/1,344m), allow five hours and another three for the descent. Make sure you are properly equipped.
Little remains of the fort, built in the reign of William III, that gave the town its name, but you can learn about the local past in the **West Highland Museum** in Cameron Square (*closed*: Sundays). The ruins of 13th-century **Inverlochy Castle** (*open*: April to September) are just 2 miles (3.2km) northeast of Fort William. Local legend insists that it is the site of a Pictish city.
Twelve miles (20km) west of Fort William, on the A830, is the **Glenfinnan Monument**, marking the spot where Bonnie Prince Charlie raised his standard on 19 April 1745 at the

ARGYLL, LOCHABER AND THE INNER ISLES MAP

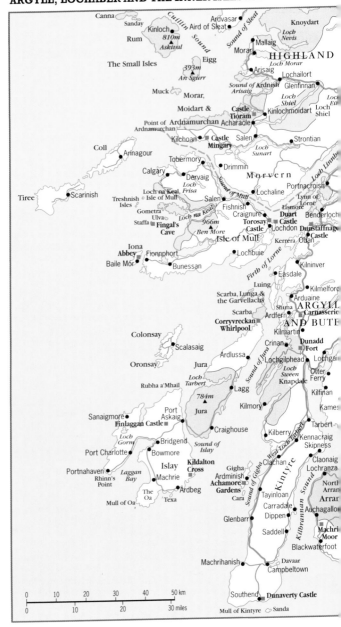

Canna
Sanday
Kinloch
Rum
810m
Askival
Cuillin Sound
Ardvasar
Aird of Sleat
Sound of Sleat
Knoydart
Loch Nevis
Mallaig
Morar
HIGHLAND
The Small Isles
Eigg
393m
An Sgurr
Arisaig
Lochailort
Sound of Ardnish Arisaig
Glenfinnan
Loch Morar
Muck
Morar,
Moidart &
Castle Tioram
Acharacle
Kinlochmoidart
Loch Shiel
Loch Eil
Loch Shiel
Point of Ardnamurchan
Ardnamurchan
Kilchoan
Castle Mingary
Salen
Loch Sunart
Strontian
Coll
Arinagour
Tobermory
Calgary
Dervaig
Drimnin
Morvern
Loch Linnh
Loch na Keal, *Loch Frisa*
Isle of Mull
Lochaline
Portnacroish
Tiree
Scarinish
Treshnish Isles
Salen
Fishnish
Sound of Mull
Lynn of Lorne
Lismore
Gometra
Ulva
Staffa
Fingal's Cave
Loch na Keal
966m
Ben More
Craignure
Torosay Castle
Duart Castle
Lochdon
Benderloch
Dunstaffnage Castle
Oban
Isle of Mull
Kerrera
Iona Abbey
Fionnphort
Baile Mór
Bunessan
Lochbuie
Firth of Lorne
Kilninver
Easdale
Luing
Kilmelford
Scarba, Lunga & the Garvellachs
Arduaine
Shuna
ARGYLL
Scarba
Ardfern
Carnasserie
Corryvreckan Whirlpool
Kilmartin
AND BUTE
Colonsay
Scalasaig
Crinan
Dunadd Fort
Lochgilphead
Lochgai
Ardlussa
Jura
Loch Sween
Knapdale
Otter Ferry
Oronsay
Loch Tarbert
Kilfinan
Rubha a'Mhail
784m
Jura
Lagg
Kilmory
Kames
Sanaigmore
Port Askaig
Craighouse
Kilberry
Tarbert
Finlaggan Castle
Loch Gorm
Bridgend
Sound of Islay
Kennacraig
Skipness
Port Charlotte
Bowmore
Islay
Kildalton Cross
Gigha
Clachan
Claonaig
Lochranza
Portnahaven
Rhinn's Point
Laggan Bay
Machrie
Ardminish
Achamore Gardens
Cara
West Loch Tarbert
Nort Arran
Arrar
Auchagallo
Mull of Oa
Texa
Ardbeg
Tayinloan
Carradale
Sound of Gigha
Kilbrannan Sound
Machri Moor
Glenbarr
Dippen
Saddell
Kintyre
Blackwaterfoot
Machrihanish
Davaar
Campbeltown
Southend
Dunaverty Castle
Mull of Kintyre
Sanda

0   10   20   30   40   50 km
0   10   20   30 miles

start of his campaign which was to end in the carnage and humiliation of Culloden (see page 71).

(see page 71)

◆◆
GIGHA
This small island off the coast of Kintyre (connected by ferry from Kennacraig and Tayinloan) has one of the region's unsung treasures in the 50-acre (20ha) garden at Achamore, which hosts an immense range of flowering trees.
Open: daily.

◆◆
GLENCOE
between Kingshouse and Loch Leven
This wild and beautiful glen, overlooked by rugged mountains, is the scene of one of the most infamous incidents in Scottish history and strikes even the casual visitor with a strange chill. The story is told in the Visitors' Centre near the foot of the glen.

The Glencoe Massacre
On 13 February 1692, men of the Campbell clan massacred 38 members of the Macdonald clan, indiscriminately attacking women, children and the sick. William III backed this slaughter in the hope it would discourage doubts about the legitimacy of Queen Mary on the throne in place of James VII (James II to the English).
What made the plot so notorious was its cynical abuse of the laws of Highland hospitality, for the Campbells had been drinking and eating with the Macdonalds just hours before.

◆◆
INVERARAY AND LOCH FYNE

Loch Fyne is an enormous sea loch stretching from the Argyll mountains to the sea north of Arran. **Crarae Glen Garden** (*open*: daily), with 50 acres (20ha) of shrubs and rhododendrons, has wonderful views over the loch. On the northwest shore is the elegant 18th-century town of Inveraray. Do not miss the **Jail** with evocative tableau scenes. Imposing **Inveraray Castle** (*open*: April to October), the home of the Campbell Dukes of Argyll, is packed with treasures.

◆◆
IONA

The tiny holy island of Iona can be reached by ferry from Fionnphort on the Ross of Mull or on an excursion from Oban. Cars are not allowed on the island. In 563, St Columba and 12 companions arrived from Ireland, founded a monastery and began to spread

Iona – burial place of both Macbeth and Duncan

Christianity to the pagan Picts. The Iona monastery became the mother house of the Celtic church in Scotland and England. The community was raided many times by Vikings, but survived and grew in reputation and honour until all of its buildings were dismantled during the Reformation. Extensive restoration work began in the 1890s and still continues today under the auspices of the National Trust for Scotland.

◆◆◆
ISLAY AND JURA

Islay, the most southerly of the Hebrides, is reached by ferry from Kennacraig, Kintyre. Its northern hills give way to surprisingly fertile, rolling farmland on the southwest coast. The island has good trout and salmon fishing, a popular golf course at Machrie and plenty of historic sights, including the 9th-century Celtic cross at **Kildalton** and the ruins of **Finlaggan Castle**. But Islay's fame rests on its selection of malt whiskies, with their distinctive smoky peatyness,

Medieval tomb-tops at Kilmartin

made in eight distilleries. Rugged **Jura**, a haven for deer and birds, is just a 10-minute crossing from Port Askaig on Islay. It was in seclusion here that George Orwell wrote *1984*. There is only one road and one hotel (in the village of **Craighouse**). At the island's northern tip you can view **Corryvreckan whirlpool**, but like much of Jura, it can only be reached on foot.

◆◆
KILMARTIN
5 miles (8km) north of Lochgilphead
Dunadd, a rock hillfort near Kilmartin, may have been an ancient capital of Argyll. Carved on the hill are a boar and ancient Irish writing. In the graveyard of **Kilmartin Church** is a famous collection of preaching crosses and stones. Below the village, prehistoric burial cairns lead to the Temple Wood stone circle.

Boat Trips from Mallaig
The fishing port of **Mallaig** is the departure point for ferries to the Inner Isles; some are easy day trips. Note that only the Skye boat accepts cars.
Eigg's main feature is a strange hill, the Sgurr, consisting of black, glassy pitchstone. **Muck**, the smallest island in the group, is named after the Gaelic for 'pig', because of its shape. It is more easily reached from Eigg than from Mallaig.

Lozenge-shaped **Rum** has the most spectacular scenery. Its volcanic mountain cluster peaks in Askival and rises to a height of 2,659 feet (810m). The island once had over 400 inhabitants, but the 19th-century Clearances forced the entire population to America. Rum is now owned by Scottish Natural Heritage.
On the island of **Canna** iron deposits in the basalt of Compass Hill are said to disturb ships' compasses.

MULL

accessible by ferry from Oban to Craignure or from Lochaline to Fishnish

Mull is an island of rocky cliffs and sandy beaches, lonely moors and high mountains, but most of all a land of undulating meadows with crofts and small farms. Sights include two castles near Craignure: **Duart Castle** (*open*: daily, May to September) and 19th-century **Torosay Castle**, outstanding for its Italian-style terraced gardens (*open*: house: April to October; gardens: all year).

Tobermory, is the island's main town. Generations of treasure-hunters have sought the *Florida*, a galleon from the Spanish Armada that sank in the bay in 1588. Individual objects have been recovered over the years. From Mull you can also visit the isle of Staffa, site of the famous Fingal's Cave.

Colourful Tobermory, Mull

OBAN

Oban has good sea-angling, golf and pony-trekking and a few sandy beaches, while ferries ply to the islands of Mull, Iona, Coll, Tiree, Colonsay and Lismore. There is plenty to see in and around the town, starting with the seafront and the ruined **Dunollie Castle**. Oban is overlooked by the curious unfinished **McCaig's Folly** (1897). An imitation of Rome's Colosseum, it was started by a banker as a work creation scheme for the local unemployed. Other attractions include the **Oban Glassworks**, the **Highland Pottery**, the **World in Miniature** toy and model display and the **Oban Distillery** (book in advance for a tour). Just outside the town is the **Oban Rare Breeds Farm**, while **Dunstaffnage Castle** (*open*: daily, April to September), 2 miles (3km) north, is an impressive 13th-century fortress.

ACCOMMODATION AND EATING OUT

The Mainland
Loch Lomond and Loch Fyne
The **Ardlui Hotel**, **Ardlui** (tel: 01301 704243) is a small, friendly country hotel situated at the northern tip of Loch Lomond. At Loch Fyne you can enjoy a seafood feast with spectacular views at the **Loch Fyne Oyster Bar**. The **Kilfinan Hotel**, Kilfinan (tel: 01700 821201), in the hamlet near the loch, has 16th-century vaults and good food. **Crinan Hotel**, Crinan (by Lochgilphead) (tel: 01546 830261) is famous for its delicious seafood which is brought in daily.

Oban Area
There are so many hotels, guest houses and B & Bs in Oban that you might prefer to take a look before you book. Largely genteel and old-fashioned, they include the **Caledonian Hotel** (tel: 01631 563133), one of the larger hotels overlooking the harbour, and the **Argyll Hotel** (tel: 01631 562353) with slightly younger clientele and a bit cheaper. **Knipoch Hotel** in Kilninver just outside Oban (tel: 01852 316251) is a luxury hotel overlooking Loch Feochan which has won awards for its food (closed January).

Mallaig Area
The **West Highland Hotel** (tel: 01687 462210) is family-run and has good views to the islands (*open*: April to October). The recently rebuilt **Glenuig Inn** at Lochailort (tel: 01687 470208), set in a lovely sandy bay, offers very good food.

Oban, with McCaig's Folly

Fort William Area
Inverlochy Castle Hotel, Torlundy (tel: 01397 702177) is extremely expensive and comfortable. **Nevis Bank**, Fort William (tel: 01397 705721) is popular with outdoor enthusiasts. The **Glengarry Castle Hotel**, Invergarry (tel: 01809 501254) is a quiet base for exploring the Northern Highlands (*open*: April to October). Head for Fort William pier for seafood.

The Islands
Arran
Auchrannie Country House Hotel, Brodick (tel: 01770 302234), is a 19th-century mansion close to the golf course and offering excellent food. **Invercloy Hotel**, Brodick (tel: 01770 302225), is informal and friendly, opposite a safe, sandy beach. **Kinloch Hotel** (tel: 01770 860444), overlooking the sea at Blackwaterfoot, is a modern hotel with many facilities.

Bute
Guildford Court, Rothesay (tel: 01700 503770), has hotel rooms and self-catering apartments at moderate prices.
Bayview Hotel, Rothesay (tel: 01700 502339), near the pier, offers reasonable food.

Islay
The **Machrie Hotel** (tel: 01496 302310) is next to a golf course.

Mull
Mull has plenty of small, traditional hotels including the **Western Isles Hotel** at Tobermory (tel: 01688 302012) with excellent views and friendly service (open March to October). **Ardfenaig House** at Bunessan (tel: 01681 700210) is a quiet comfortable country hotel with excellent food (open May to September).
Druimnacroish Country House Hotel at Dervaig (tel: 01688 400274), though more expensive, is very comfortable. For an overnight stop on Iona, the **Abbey** (tel: 01681 700404) has 23 rooms, simple food and no licence.

Iona ferry – see page 56

PERTHSHIRE, ANGUS AND FIFE MAP

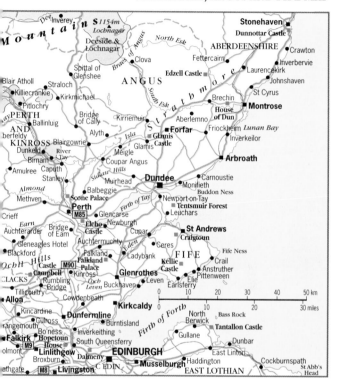

PERTHSHIRE, ANGUS AND FIFE

The area covered here is ranged around the Firths of Forth and Tay, a pair of wide tidal inlets that cut deep into the east coast of Scotland. Angus and Fife have broad swathes of farmland, some of the richest in all Britain, while the shores of the Firths are lined with market towns proud of privileges long established by royal charters. This area was the centre of the old kingdom of Scotland when Stirling, Perth, St Andrews and Arbroath hosted national assemblies and royal courts, but the industrial revolution shifted the balance of power and population south, to the Glasgow-Edinburgh axis where it remains. Civilised, although rather old-fashioned, the area is visited today for the palaces, cathedrals and abbeys, old ports and tower houses – and for the fine beaches and golf links.

Blair Castle – rebuilt many times since the 13th century

◆
ANSTRUTHER

Anstruther comprises Anstruther Easter, Cellerdyke and Anstruther Wester, each once with its own kirk, mercat cross (where proclamations were made), tolbooth, castle and harbour. A complex of historic buildings on the harbourhead at Anstruther Easter house the **Scottish Fisheries Museum** (*open*: daily). There is an aquarium, and galleries devoted to sailing, whaling, the role of women on shore, as well as real boats. (The neighbouring harbour at Pittenweem still supports a working fishing fleet.) In summer it is possible to organise a boat trip from Anstruther to the bird sanctuary on the Isle of May.

◆
ARBROATH

The great 12th-century sandstone **Abbey** stands in picturesque ruins (*open*: daily). The gatehouse, sacristry and Abbot's House give scale and you can see some intact vaults. The nearby beaches give the town a resort air in the summer; the fishing port has given it international culinary status as the originator of 'Arbroath Smokies' – split, smoked haddock on the skin. To the north is the hamlet of **St Vigeans** arranged around its prominent church. A museum (*open*: daily) houses over 40 Pictish, Celtic, and early Christian carved stones.

♦♦♦
BLAIR CASTLE

Blair Atholl, between Perth and Inverness
The white walls and turrets of Blair Castle are enclosed in a park-like garden amid the beautiful Atholl hills. The castle is the seat of the Duke of Atholl, the only person under the monarchy allowed to retain a private army, the 100-strong Atholl Highlanders. Following the last Duke's death in March 1996, however, the estate has been left to a trust. The castle has an exceptional collection of antiquities, with many treasures, notably some rare 17th-century Scottish furniture. Three miles (5km) away (signposted) are the gorge, bridges and waterfall of **Bruar**.
Castle open: daily, April to October.
Closed: Sunday afternoon.

♦♦
CRAIL

Crail is the most picturesque of the half dozen ancient fishing ports that dot that part of the Fife coast known as the East Neuk. It is a summer resort and an artists' colony, and still maintains a small flotilla of fishing boats in its handsome stone harbour. The 16th-century tolbooth (behind which is the town museum), the mercat cross, a fine 12th-century church and the broad tree-lined Marketgate recall the burgh's more prosperous centuries and its famous Sunday market. A road leads east to the lighthouse and golf links, past **Balcomie Castle**,

where Mary of Guise, mother of Mary Queen of Scots, spent her first night in Scotland.

♦♦
CRIEFF

A small town surrounded by the beautiful Perthshire hills, this is a good place from which to explore the central highlands. Drummond Castle, whose unrivalled formal garden featured in the film *Rob Roy*, is near by (*open*: May to September afternoons).

♦♦
CULROSS

7 miles (11km) west of Dunfermline
This small coastal town in western Fife has been superbly conserved by the National Trust for Scotland. It is a time-capsule of a 17th-century burgh which prospered on coal and salt. The cobbled streets have crowstepped houses with terracotta pantiled roofs typical of Fife. The town's **tolbooth** puts on free video shows in the basement. Beside it is the restored **palace** (*open*: daily) of Sir George Bruce, the local landowner. **Bishop Leighton's Study** (*open*: weekend afternoons, April to October) is the name given to the corbelled 17th-century townhouse by the mercat cross. The Abbey church at the top of Kirk Street, alongside some monastic fragments, functions as the parish church.

♦♦
DOUNE AND DUNBLANE

These neighbouring towns lie just north of Stirling. **Doune**, a tidy unpretentious place, used to be famous for its pistols and its livestock markets. On the southern edge of the town, beside the site of a Roman fort at the junction of the Ardoch Water and River Teith, is **Doune Castle**, a 14th-century royal fortress with a Z-shape plan formed from its massive gatehouse and great halls half enclosed in a curtain wall (*open*: daily; *closed*: October to March Thursday afternoon and Friday). Tiny **Dunblane** to the east, beside the Allan Water, is dignified by its fine Gothic **cathedral**. The tower is 12th-century; the splendid nave, 210 feet (64m) from west door to altar, was built by Bishop Clement (1233–58). A small museum has been established in the old Deanery.

DUNDEE
Scotland's fourth city sits beneath the Sidlaw Hills along the north bank of the Firth of Tay. Beside the modern road bridge linking Dundee to the northern Fife shore is the Victorian railway bridge, successor to one destroyed with a trainload of passengers in a winter storm in 1879, an event recorded in the unintentionally comic verse of William McGonagall. The medieval town was completely remade in the furious industrial boom of the early 19th century. In the city centre in Albert Square is the splendidly Gothic building of the **McManus Galleries** (closed Sundays). Just southeast is the **Howff**, an atmospheric Victorian necropolis beside the Barrack

Street natural history museum. To the east of City Square, which is overlooked by the imposing Caird Hall, the cathedral and the three churches under one roof that comprise City Churches, is the old harbour area. Victoria dock has been developed as an open air nautical museum and houses *Discovery*, the ship used by Captain Scott's famous Antarctic expedition and HMS *Unicorn*, a 46-gun frigate (*open*: weekdays, April to October).

DUNFERMLINE
Dunfermline, the 'auld grey town', is best known as the birthplace of Andrew Carnegie. He returned to Scotland after making a colossal fortune in the United States and used much of his wealth to enrich his home town, among other things giving the citizens the wooded glen of Pittencrieff Park. The first of many Carnegie libraries was opened here. Dunfermline is also famous for its **abbey** (*open*: daily; *closed*: October to March Thursday afternoon, Friday, and Sunday morning), the burial place of Robert the Bruce, Malcolm III Canmore and his saintly Queen, Margaret.
Around the abbey church are the ruins of the old monastic and royal apartments. The tower and eastern end were rebuilt in the 19th century to serve as a parish church. The 12th-century nave at the west end, with its Romanesque columns, arches and zigzag chevrons, is particularly attractive.

Shop window in Falkland

◆◆
EDZELL CASTLE
6 miles (9.5km) due north of Brechin
This ruined castle, a tower house extended into a 16th-century mansion, is remarkable for its walled garden, the Pleasance, laid out in 1604. Sculptural reliefs on the walls illustrate the Cardinal Virtues, Planetary Deities and Liberal Arts.
Open: daily.
Closed: October to March, Thursday afternoon and Friday.

◆◆
FALKLAND
15 miles (24km) southeast of Perth
The unspoiled village of Falkland beneath the Lomond hills preserves at its centre elegant **Falkland Palace** (completed in 1542), the favourite retreat of four generations of Stewart monarchs. The Marquis of Bute partially restored the palace (saving the carved and painted wooden fixtures) in the late 19th century.
Open: daily, April to October.

◆◆
GLAMIS
12 miles (19km) north of Dundee
Turreted **Glamis Castle** (guided tours daily, May to mid October), its central medieval core extended by Victorian wings, stands stern and serene amid its deer park and tree-lined avenues. The Macbeth connections are Shakespearian fiction; other weird tales are of the ghost of a Lady Glamis burned as a witch, and of an imprisoned beast-heir. In recent times Glamis was the childhood home of the Queen Mother and the birthplace of Princess Margaret. The guided tour takes in the magnificent 17th-century reception rooms, painted chapel, vaulted drawing room, restored library and dining-room, Duncan's Hall (the oldest section) and the archives in the towers. Kirkwynd Cottages, near the entrance to the grounds, contain the **Angus Folk Museum** (*open:* daily, May to October).

Seven miles (11km) west, in the schoolhouse of Meigle village, is an important collection of 25 carved stones – the **Meigle Stones** – which bridge the cultural gap between Pictish and Celtic early Christian symbolism (*open*: weekdays).

KELLIE CASTLE AND BALCASKIE HOUSE
3 miles (5km) northwest of Anstruther
Built between the 14th and 17th centuries, **Kellie Castle**, with its irregular corbelled corner turrets and stepped gables, is a classic Lowlands round tower house. Just south is **Balcaskie House**, the imposing 17th-century mansion of the Anstruther family. The house's fame rests on the splendid Italianate terraces of its formal garden, the earliest in Scotland. *Castle and house open*: May to September afternoons; October weekends only.

LEUCHARS
between Dundee and St Andrews
This coastal village is worth visiting for **Earlshall Castle**, a well-restored 16th-century tower house, embellished with gatehouse and gardens at the turn of the century (summer opening hours); and the 12th-century eastern apse of the **parish church**, one of the finest examples of the Romanesque in Scotland. From Leuchars, a road leads northeast through the pine woods of Tentsmuir Forest Nature Reserve to unpopulated Kinshaldy beach.

LOCH TAY
The serene 14-mile (22.5km) long Loch Tay, below the summit of Ben Lawers to its north, snakes its way northeast from Killin to Kenmore. The village of **Killin** lies between the falls of the Lochay and Docharty burns. Ruined **Finlarig Castle** is half a mile (1km) north, a Campbell stronghold. At the east end of the loch is a 1774 bridge, Taymouth Castle, with its arcadian outbuildings, and the 'model' village of **Kenmore**, now a resort for watersports enthusiasts. Seven miles (11km) east, the market town of **Aberfeldy** is approached by way of its grand 'Wade' bridge. Near by are Castle Menzies (a 16th-century tower house); the old Kirk of Weem with a pair of Celtic crosses; and 17th-century St Mary's with its painted ceiling.

PERTH AND SCONE PALACE
In a pleasant setting of parks beside the Tay, Perth is usefully sited as a central road and railway base for exploring Scotland. Attractions in the vicinity, including romantic ruined Dunkeld Cathedral, Elcho and Huntingtower Castles and the world's tallest beech hedge at Meikleour House. Nearest of all to Perth is **Scone Palace**, one of the great treasure-houses of Scotland. It was built by James Wyatt in Gothic style at the beginning of the 19th century on the foundations of an old abbey. Its

state rooms contain fine English and French furnishings. The grounds contain the chapel-crowned Moot Hill, associated with the Stone of Destiny (Stone of Scone), which is currently in Westminster Abbey in London but due to be returned to Scotland in the near future. *Open:* weekdays April to October.

◆
PITLOCHRY
30 miles (48km) north of Perth
Once a health centre for city-bound Victorians, Pitlochry now hosts a summer arts festival in the fine Festival Theatre, and is a convenient base from which to explore nearby attractions such as the **Queen's View** up Loch Tummel and the Salmon

Ladder on the River Tummel. Further west is the awesome glacier-gouged 10-mile trench of **Loch Rannoch**, overlooked to its south by the conical peak of Schiehallion (3,554 feet/1,083m).

◆◆
ST ANDREWS
This Fife market town and summer beach resort is renowned for its university (the first in Scotland) and its golf course. Visitors are more immediately aware of the towering ruins of its pre-Reformation cathedral. Just seaward of the cathedral precinct wall lie the exposed foundations of the first Celtic church (St Mary of the Rock)

St Andrews from St Rule's Tower

which was replaced by the tall square tower of the Catholic **Church of St Regulus** (or St Rule) in the 12th century. Beside the tower extends the enormous ruined nave of the 14th-century **cathedral**. Further west are the cliff-perched ruins of the **bishop's castle**, and below it the Martyrs' Monument, which stands directly above the grand **Royal and Ancient Club** (along with the US Golf Association, the ruling body for the rules of world golf). It overlooks the Old Course and a golfing museum. There is more to see in the medieval town and shopping district: university buildings of the 15th and 16th centuries, West Port gate, the spire of Holy Trinity Church and the ruins of the Blackfriars chapel mingled with fine townhouses and secretive wynds (lanes). Out-of-town attractions include **Craigtoun Country Park**, 16th-century **Scotstarvit Tower**, and Edwardian **Hill of Tarvit** – both near the village of Ceres, which contains the **Fife Folk Museum**. *Cathedral, museum and castle open*: daily; other local sites open afternoons April to October.

◆◆
STIRLING

This fine town is at the centre of Scotland, both geographically and historically. The grey walls of **Stirling Castle** (*open*: daily) crown the volcanic crag that bestrides the narrow pass between the tidal Forth and the Gargunnock hills, connecting the northern and southern halves of the country. Possession of the castle was the symbolic key to

Scotland. The **Wallace Monument** (1870), high up on the eastern edge of the town, commemorates the 13th-century resistance hero William Wallace. It contains a visitor centre with displays on local heroes (*open*: daily). On the other side of town is the **Bannockburn Heritage Centre** (*open*: daily, April to October) commemorating Robert the Bruce's victory over Edward II in 1314. On your way you will see, in a loop of the river, Gothic Cambuskenneth Priory. Back in the old town, walk along St John Street with the Church of the Holy Rude and the former military hospital called Argyll's Lodging below the double skin of castle gates. The castle walls enclose 18th-century artillery batteries, gardens, a Royal Chapel, and the 16th-century palace built by the Stewart Kings.

The Trossachs

A beautiful combination of hills, burns, woods and lochs, the Trossachs (meaning the 'bristly country') stretches from Callander to the shores of Loch Lomond with the resort town of Aberfoyle as its centre. Its accessibility is perhaps its undoing – the Trossachs is one of the most visited areas in Scotland. Literary associations are strong. This was the territory of the MacGregor clan and their chief Rob Roy, immortalised by Sir Walter Scott, whose poem *The Lady of the Lake* also vividly evokes the region to its readers. A favourite outing is a cruise on Loch Katrine on the vintage steamer *Sir Walter Scott*.

ACCOMMODATION AND EATING OUT

Perthshire, Angus and Dundee

The **Gleneagles Hotel** (tel: 01764 662231) has an international reputation and a central position outside Auchterarder. Great for sports fanatics and business people. For half the price you could stay at **Kinloch House** near Blairgowrie (tel: 01250 884237), where excellent food and service are set off by elegant surroundings. Blairgowrie has several other good hotels. In Angus, 6-bedroomed **Castleton House**, 3 miles (4.8km) from Glamis, is a good bet (tel: 01307 840340). For Perth, try the **Murrayshall Country House** at Scone (tel:

In the Trossachs

01738 551171). At Kenmore the **Kenmore Hotel** (tel: 01887 830205) provides a base for exploring the central Highlands. Dundee has the **Swallow** (tel: 01382 641122), set in a former baronial hall, and the modern **Angus Thistle** (tel: 01382 226874).

Stirlingshire

Beside the River Teith at Callander is the **Roman Camp Hotel** (tel: 01877 330003). **Cromlix House** at Kinbuck, Dunblane (tel: 01786 822125), is more expensive but is conveniently central.

Close to Stirling Castle and with superb views of Stirling and its surroundings, is the **Stirling Highland** (tel: 01786 475444), which is converted from a high school.

Fife

St Andrews boasts two fine hotels, the **Forte Heritage Rusack's** on Pilmour Links (tel: 01334 474321) and the **St Andrews Old Course Hotel** (tel: 01334 474371) in the middle of the Golf Course. Cheaper hotels abound on The Scores.

Fife is the area for good eating. Anstruther's **Cellar Restaurant**, 24 East Green Street (tel: 01333 310378), uses excellent fresh ingredients from Pittenweem combined with traditional French cooking. **Ostlers Close** at 25 Bonnygate, Cupar (tel: 01334 655574) has a welcome bias towards vegetables. The **Peat Inn** on the junction of the B940 and B941 about 5 miles (8km) southwest of St Andrews near Cupar is a centre of culinary excellence (tel: 01334 840206).

THE NORTHEAST

The fertile garden-filled coastal plain of the northeast of Scotland is a striking counterpoint to the mountain landscapes south and west. Aberdeen and Inverness are twin provincial capitals of this plain. The landscape here is much softer than the dramatic west coast. It builds up slowly from coastal farmland to inner ranges of moorland, dressed in outcrops of woodland before climbing up to the high rounded scree slope summits of the Cairngorms. We have divided the area covered in this chapter into two parts, based on Inverness and Aberdeen, with the Spey valley as a frontier.

INVERNESS

Its strategically important position at the northern head of the Great Glen has given the 'Capital of the Highlands' an important place in Scotland's history. Tradition records a missionary visit from St Columba, while invasions (by the Norse, the English, Robert the Bruce, the Lord of the Isles) and Jacobite rebellions filled the annals of the city's history although few tangible remnants of this past survive. Most of the town dates from the 19th century, when Inverness expanded thanks to the railway and Telford's Caledonian Canal. The Cathedral of St Andrew by the River Ness is Victorian Gothic. Across the river is the 19th-century castle. Today, Inverness is said to be one of Europe's fastest growing cities.

◆
AVIEMORE AND THE CAIRNGORMS
33 miles (53km) south of Inverness
An unattractive creation of the 1960s, Aviemore is nevertheless a popular centre for hill walking in the Cairngorm mountains in the summer and for skiing in the winter. (For more details on the Cairngorms area, see the **Peace and Quiet** section, starting on page 93.)
A pleasant excursion is the steam train ride to Boat of Garten. In the Aviemore Centre you can enjoy a whisky centre, indoor sports, and discothèques.

Loch Ness and 'Nessie'
Scotland's largest loch, though impressive, has little of the charm and serpentine movement found in many less celebrated lochs. Its fame rests solely on the legend of 'Nessie', the much sought, seldom seen monster believed to reside in its waters.
Visit the **Loch Ness Monster Exhibition** at Drumnadrochit to see what are claimed to be photographs of Nessie and to learn how hi-tech methods are being used to try to solve the mystery.
There are good views from **Urquhart Castle**, on a rocky cliff above the loch.
At the southern end of Loch Ness is the little town of **Fort Augustus** on the Caledonian Canal. The Hanoverian fort which gave the town its name has been absorbed into a 19th-century Benedictine monastery.

◆◆
CAWDOR CASTLE
about 14 miles (22km) east of Inverness

The present castle, with origins in the 14th century, has nothing to do with Macbeth. The original keep remains; the rest is mainly from the 17th century. Inside, you can see Jacobean rooms and Flemish tapestries, including some after designs by Rubens.

Open: daily, May to September.

◆◆
CULLODEN BATTLEFIELD
6 miles (9.5km) east of Inverness

The last battle on British soil was fought here on 16 April 1746, remembered as one of the bloodiest engagements between England and Scotland. It marked the end of the attempt by Prince Charles Edward

The Aviemore ski lift takes summer visitors close to the summit of Cairn Gorm

Stuart (Bonnie Prince Charlie or the Young Pretender) to gain the British throne from the Hanoverian George II. The King's younger son was nicknamed 'Butcher Cumberland' for his cruel pursuit of his enemies after the battle. The Visitor Centre tells the whole story. The graves of the different clans are marked by stones and monuments, and you can follow the front lines of each army on marked paths.

◆◆
KINGUSSIE
halfway between Inverness and Pitlochry

Pronounced 'Kinusie', this

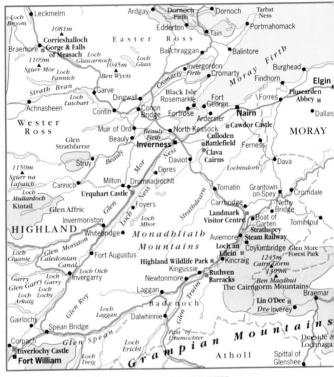

charming town has just one main street but plenty of lovely walks in the vicinity. The **Highland Folk Museum** (*open:* daily, April to October; November to March weekdays only) has indoor and outdoor exhibitions with traditional houses and working buildings. On the other side of the River Spey is the ruin of the grim **Ruthven Barracks**, built in 1718 to hold the Highlands in check and destroyed in 1746 after the Jacobite rebellion.

ABERDEEN

The 'Granite City' is Scotland's third largest town. The oil boom of the 1970s brought new buildings and mighty oil-rig vessels, but Aberdeen's more dignified Georgian and Victorian past is still apparent, based on well-established prosperity. An important port, it has long been a busy commercial centre.

The city's architectural gems include the oldest medieval bridge in Scotland, the **Brig**

THE NORTHEAST MAP

O'Balgownie over the River
Don and, in the tranquil area
known as Old Aberdeen,
St Machar's Cathedral, the
world's only granite cathedral.
The main city is centred on
Broad Street and Union Street
with university buildings,
markets and museums. The
tolbooth here is the town jail,
built in 1627 (tours by
appointment). See too **The
Aberdeen Art Gallery and
Museum** (art of the 18th–20th
centuries); **Provost Ross's

House**, Aberdeen's oldest
building, dating from 1594 and
now a maritime museum with
displays on fishing history, the
tea clippers of the 19th-century
China trade and recent oil
exploration; and **Provost
Skene's House** (social history).
Duthie Park Winter Gardens
are a tropical paradise with
birds, fish, turtles, cacti and
palm trees. For a bit of local
colour, take in Aberdeen's fish
market, which gets under way
at around 04.30hrs.

◆◆
BALMORAL
halfway between Braemar and Ballater
Bought by Queen Victoria in 1852, the old castle was considered too small and today's Balmoral mansion was commissioned by her husband, Prince Albert. It is still a favourite holiday home of the Royal Family.
Grounds open: May to July Monday to Saturday.

◆
BRAEMAR
Gloriously situated among the Deeside hills, some 9 miles (14.5km) from Balmoral, Braemar is ever popular as a holiday centre. Its 17th-century L-plan **castle** was built as a hunting lodge, and served as a Hanoverian fort. The **Braemar Gathering**, held on the first Saturday in September, is the premier event of its kind, regularly attended by the Royal Family. There are traditional games such as tossing the caber (a pinewood pole up to 20 feet/7m long), and piping and dancing contests.
Six miles (9.6km) west of Braemar is the beautiful **Linn O'Dee**, where the River Dee forms a succession of cascades and rocky pools.

◆◆◆
CRAIGIEVAR CASTLE ✓

26 miles (42km) west of Aberdeen
The fairytale pink castle of Craigievar stands peacefully in the Don Valley. Its walls rise plainly, only to sprout a playful summit of conical corner towers, a sky-high balustrade, Renaissance domes and fancy gables. It is virtually untouched since completion in the 17th century when William Forbes, a prosperous Aberdonian merchant (nicknamed Danzig Willie), gave a master mason a free hand and a full purse.
Open: castle: daily, May to September (guided tours); grounds: daily, all year.

◆◆◆
CRATHES CASTLE ✓

10 miles (18km) southwest of Aberdeen
Jacobean Crathes has been restored following a fire in 1966 which burned down Victorian extensions. The interior is renowned for remarkable, painted ceilings in the Room of the Nine Nobles, the Room of the Muses and the Room of the Green Lady. The ghost of a lady dressed in green is said to

Craigievar Castle

haunt the castle. The eight linked gardens, each one different, are enclosed within 300-year-old yew hedges and, with their arches, avenues and prospects, provide constant surprises.
Open: castle: daily, April to October; garden: daily, all year.

Crathes Castle

DUFF HOUSE
Banff
Recently opened as an outpost of the National Galleries of Scotland, this is a handsome mansion by William Adam. The house has recently been conserved and is now open as an art gallery.
Open: daily.

DRUM CASTLE
7 miles (11km) southwest of Aberdeen off the A93
In the Old Wood of Drum – a remnant of the ancient Caledonian Forest – is Drum Castle, a 13th-century keep with 12-foot- (4m) thick walls, and an attached Jacobean mansion housing a collection of portraits, silver and furniture.
Open: castle: May to September every afternoon; April and October weekends only; grounds: all year.

FYVIE CASTLE
about 25 miles (40km) northwest of Aberdeen
Built in the 13th century, Fyvie has been enlarged by its various resident families, who added towers and halls to this great baronial pile. Its present look and interior are due to American steel tycoon

Alexander Forbes-Leith, who bought the estate in 1889 and filled it with treasures, including portraits by Gainsborough, Opie and Raeburn, and some beautiful furniture.
Open: daily, April to September, weekend afternoons in October.

STONEHAVEN AND DUNNOTTAR CASTLE
about 15 miles (24km) south of Aberdeen
The old fishing port and resort of Stonehaven is increasingly filled with yachts in summer. The 16th-century town, with the old tolbooth (now a local museum), is ranged around the harbour; the 18th-century new town consists of spacious streets surrounding the Market Square.
Just south of Stonehaven, on a cliff-girt promontory, are the impressive ruins of **Dunnottar Castle**. Dunnottar was founded back in the 5th century when it was a lonely outpost of Roman Christianity.
Castle ruins open: weekdays all year, also summer weekends.

ACCOMMODATION AND EATING OUT

Aberdeen
Copthorne Hotel, 122 Huntly Street (tel: 01224 630404), is conveniently central with a good restaurant called Poachers. **Imperial Hotel**, Stirling Street (tel: 01224 589101), combines old-fashioned elegance with a central location.
Mr G's, 74 Chapel Street, is a popular wine bar and restaurant with an easy-going atmosphere. **Gerards**, 50 Chapel Street, serves excellent food in a conservatory-style dining room.

Balmoral and Braemar
Raemoir House Hotel, Raemoir (tel: 01330 824884), combines old-world interiors with modern facilities.

Elgin
Mansion House Hotel, The Haugh, Elgin (tel: 01343 548811). Comfortable and quiet.

Banff
Fife Lodge Hotel (tel: 01261 812436). Overlooks the River Deveron.

Inverness
The nicest hotels are just outside the town: **Bunchrew House Hotel**, Bunchrew (tel: 01463 234917), is a small, turreted 16th-century mansion overlooking the Beauly Firth. You must reserve one of the six bedrooms. **Culloden House Hotel** (tel: 01463 790461) offers grand luxury in a Georgian mansion with Bonnie Prince Charlie connections. Excellent food, four-poster beds – the works. In Inverness itself try the Loch Ness House Hotel (tel: 01463 231248).

Kingussie
Muckrach Lodge Hotel, Dulnain Bridge (tel: 01479 851257), is laid-back and comfortable in lovely grounds.

Loch Ness
Glenmoriston Arms Hotel (tel: 01320 351206), is a traditional inn, distinguished for serving 170 malt whiskies. **Knockie Lodge Hotel**, Whitebridge (tel: 01456 486276), is a comfortable hotel in the wilderness above Loch Ness.

Huge Highland landscapes, with Torridon village in the valley

WESTER ROSS, SKYE AND THE OUTER HEBRIDES

Windblown, remote and misty, rich in legend and traditional in its crofting lifestyle, the west coast and its outer isles capture the imagination more than any other part of Scotland. It can appear bleak and severe: its mercurial weather can show you all four seasons in as many hours and the summer midges are notoriously vicious. But just one glorious day on a Hebridean beach or hill can make you an addict for life. The region has a wealth of prehistoric remains going back as far as neolithic times. They include stone circles, burial cairns, towers and hill-forts. In the beginning of the historic period the islands were under Norse dominion, broken only in the 12th century. In the next century, the independent Lordship of the Isles was set up under a Macdonald clan chief, and lasted until 1493, when the Scottish king claimed the title.

WESTER ROSS

The mainland shore, heavily indented with long sea lochs that reflect the brooding mountains, can boast some of the most remarkable scenery in Europe.

◆◆
APPLECROSS PENINSULA

One of the most dramatic roads in the British Isles starts from the head of Loch Kishorn to twist steeply over the 2,054-foot (626m) Bealach na Ba (Pass of the Cattle) to Applecross village on the coast. Here a Celtic cross marks the site of an important 7th-century monastery. From the summit of the pass there is an awesome view back over Loch Kishorn and Loch Carron.

◆◆
EILEAN DONAN CASTLE

5 miles (8km) east of Kyle of Lochalsh
This much photographed castle stands picturesquely on an islet at the meeting of three lochs. Long a desolate ruin, it was fully restored this century. So strong was it that in 1539 the castle was held by two men and a lad against a fleet of galleys. Two large rooms are open to the

0   10   20   30   40   50 km
0   10   20   30 miles

WESTERN
ISLES

Outer Hebrides

Garenin
Carloway
Dun Carloway
Loch Roag
Breasclere
Miavaig   Great
Bernera **Callanish**
Uig

Mealasta   *Loch   Balallan
                Langavat*
          *Loch   Arivruaich
Scarp   Resort*
                        Ardvourlie
Hushinish   799m
Amhuinnsuidhe   *Clisham*
Castle
Taransay   Tarbert

South Lewis,
Harris & North Uist   Scalpay

                Borve
Pabbay   Ensay   Manish   **Harris**
Berneray   Leverburgh
Boreray *Sound of Harris* Rodel
                 Renish Point
North   Vallay
Uist Hosta   Newtonferry
Tigharry   Sollas
                    Lochmaddy
     Sound of Monach   *Little Minch*
                  Barpa Langass
Monach   Stein
Islands   Baleshare Carnish   **Dunvegan**
        Balivanich   Ronay   **Castle**
Benbecula Gramisdale   Milovaig
         Creagorry   Dunvegan
                  Wiay   Neist Point
                                 Harlosh
            ■ **Our Lady of the Isles**
South Uist   Isle
Stoneybridge   of
          ■ **Ormiclate Castle** Skye   *Loch
                                        Bracadale*
Kildonan
South Uist
Machair   Daliburgh
            Lochboisdale
Kilbride Ludag
      Sound of Barra
                Eriskay
Barra   Canna
Kisimul Castle
Vatersay Castlebay   Sanda
      ○ Muldoanich
      Sandray
      Pabbay
      Mingulay
Barra Head Berneray

Sea of the Hebrides

WESTER ROSS, SKYE AND OUTER HEBRIDES MAP

The Sligachan Hotel, Skye, dwarfed by the peaks of the Cuillins

public, as are the ramparts, offering exceptional views.
Open: daily, Easter to October.

GLENELG
The village lies west of the Shiel Bridge, on the old cattle droving road to Skye. Most visitors come to see the two best preserved brochs on the Scottish mainland, Dun Telve and Dun Troddan.
Near by, too, are the ruins of Hanoverian Bernera Barracks, and on Sandaig Bay, Gavin Maxwell's otter refuge of 'Camusfearna' described in *Ring of Bright Water*. From Glenelg, a summer car ferry goes to Kylerhea on Skye.

INVEREWE GARDENS
A barren windswept peninsula on the same latitude as Siberia would not seem a promising site for a garden. It is the warming effect of the Gulf Stream that has made possible this gorgeously laid out collection of 2,500 species of tender and hardy flowers, shrubs and trees, started in 1862 by Osgood Mackenzie.
Open: daily.

TORRIDON
The village of Torridon stands in an awesome landscape at the head of Upper Loch Torridon and at the foot of the massive slopes of Ben Liathach (the Grey One, 3,456 feet/1,054m). The area contains patches of

the ancient Caledonian forest and is managed by the National Trust for Scotland, which runs a small deer museum and walking centre.

◆
ULLAPOOL

The only town of any size on the northwest coast of Scotland, Ullapool was founded in 1788 as a centre for the herring trade. It is still a busy fishing port, and also now a centre for sailing. Pleasure boats take visitors to the charming Summer Isles, and a ferry leaves daily for Stornoway on Lewis.

SKYE

Skye is the largest and grandest Hebridean island, and the closest to the mainland, now linked by the new and controversial Skye Bridge. Those who wish to cross the water in the more traditional way can do so from Mallaig to Armadale and from Glenelg to Kylerhea.

The 'Isle of Mist' is bewilderingly irregular in shape and varied (in places bizarre) in landscape. Peninsulas and sea lochs form an indented outline, while in the centre are Portree, the capital (and only town) and the Black Cuillin Hills. Within a mere 600 square miles (1,554sq km) are high peaks and wooded valleys, wild moorland and gentle fertile farmland, sandy beaches and lowering cliffs. All of this means that it is one of the best places to enjoy a Scottish holiday.

◆◆
ARMADALE CASTLE

Built in the 19th century, the castle is now in ruin though its stable block has been restored as the **Clan Donald Centre** which attracts Macdonalds from all over the world. Videos and fine displays tell the story of the Lords of the Isles and their part in Scotland's history.
Open: centre: Easter to October; garden: daily.

◆◆
DUNVEGAN CASTLE

Since the 12th century the castle, reached by a bridge over a gully, has been the seat of the MacLeods of Skye. It contains many Clan treasures, the most famous being the Fairy Flag, an ancient piece of fine yellow Palestinian cloth. Legend has it that the Flag, when waved, can save the Clan – but only three times,

The Quiraing – once used as an inaccessible refuge for stolen cattle

The Cuillin Hills

The Cuillins, whose outline dominates Skye, provide some of the most magnificent scenery in Britain and superb climbing. Their impact is due less to sheer size than to proportion, as a result of which the peaks seem to soar to fantastic altitude and possess a rare sublimity. The climbing is serious however – not for novices – and the magnetic nature of the rock can deflect a compass needle, especially on the ridges.

and it has already twice fulfilled its promise.
Open: daily, Easter to October.

◆◆
LOCH CORUISK

You can climb from Sligachan Hotel, or walk or take a small boat from the village of Elgol, to view the most dramatic loch in Scotland, painted by Turner among many others. Enclosed within a tremendous, natural

amphitheatre of black crags, the great pool seems to absorb all light. The scene is one of overwhelming desolation and majesty.

◆
OLD MAN OF STORR
This rock pinnacle is one of Skye's landmarks. Shaped like a huge, elongated pear, it towers 165 feet (50m) above the crumbling cliffs of Trotternish.

◆◆
THE QUIRAING
This fantastic hill lies near the northern tip of Skye, a confused mass of riven cliffs, scree slopes and towering pinnacles. Its main features have been fancifully named: the 'Needle', rising to 120 feet (36m) tall; the 'Table', a huge turf-covered rock; and the 'Prison', surrounded by rocky walls. This wilderness of rocks can only be reached on foot, but the experience it provides is unique.

THE OUTER HEBRIDES
The Outer Hebrides (also called The Long Isle) are reached by ferry from Oban, Ullapool, or Uig on Skye. A remote archipelago, rocky and forbidding on the east, lined with white-sand beaches backed by lush meadowland on the west, these are the haunts of those seeking peace. The traditional crofting way of life is maintained in many places, and the manufacture of Harris tweed is a vital part of the economy.

◆
BARRA
Many think Barra (accessible by ferry from South Uist or the mainland) the most beautiful island in the world, with its miles of shimmering white beaches and rocky eastern shore. You can drive round the island in little more than an hour or cover most of it on foot in a generous day. **Castlebay**, once an important herring port, is the only town; its principal attraction is ancient Kisimul Castle on an island in the bay.

◆
ERISKAY
Reached by ferry from Ludag, South Uist, Eriskay is a sleepy place with a small industrious population and many houses only used in the summer. It was here that Bonnie Prince Charlie first landed on his fateful return from France. The island is also famous as the inspiration for Compton Mackenzie's novel *Whisky Galore*, based on an actual incident during World War II, which became a much-loved British film.

Lighthouse at Butt of Lewis, surrounded by colonies of seabirds

◆◆ LEWIS AND HARRIS

Lewis and Harris are a single landmass, the most northerly of the Hebrides. Lewis, to the north, is mainly wild moorland bog, while Harris (most famous for the tweed cloth still made there) is rocky hill country or fertile grassland.

The major sight is the evocative Bronze Age **Callanish stone circle**, beside Loch Roag on the west coast of Lewis. A central standing stone is surrounded by a ring of 13 almost equally massive stones; lines of stones lead off from the circle. Callanish was probably a temple celebrating the cycle of seasons. Other sights include **Arnol Black House Museum** (Lewis), a traditional house preserved to show a crofting way of life common only 20 years ago; **Dun Carloway** (Lewis), the finest broch in the Hebrides; and **St Clement's Church**, Rodel (Harris), 16th-century with unusual carvings. The capital of the Outer Hebrides is **Stornoway**, on the east coast of Lewis, with bars, shops and a lively art gallery.

◆ THE UISTS

North Uist, Benbecula and South Uist are joined by causeways. The ferryport of Lochmaddy, on North Uist, links the islands to Harris and Skye. Going south from here, you can see **Barpa Langass**, a tomb of the Bronze Age Beaker people, one of the finest chambered cairns in the Hebrides. Also on North Uist are **Hosta Beach** with a view towards uninhabited St Kilda, far out in the Atlantic; and **Vallay**, a tidal island off the northern tip, with the finest beaches in the Hebrides. Driving south onto South Uist, you will see the 125-foot (38m) statue of **Our Lady of the Isles** gazing out over the Atlantic. Further south is **Kildonan Museum**, with a display of Hebridean artefacts collected and maintained by local people. Near by is a cairn within a ruined croft, marking the birthplace of Flora Macdonald.

ACCOMMODATION AND EATING OUT

The Mainland

Altnaharrie Inn, on Loch Broom near Ullapool (tel: 01854 633230) is expensive but has the best cooking in Scotland. The town itself bristles with bed and breakfasts.

The Islands
Skye

There are dozens of family-run small hotels, but for something different try: **Skeabost House**, near Portree (tel: 01470 532202), grand and with its own salmon fishing; the exclusive **Kinloch Lodge** (tel: 01471 833214), run by Lord and Lady Macdonald; or, for extra isolation, take the ferry from Sconser for the **Isle of Raasay Hotel** (tel: 01478 660222).

Harris, Lewis and the Uists

Top of the range on Harris and Lewis is **Ardvourlie Castle** (tel: 01859 502307), a Victorian hunting lodge. On the west coast is the 7-bedroom **Scarista House Hotel** (tel: 01859 550277), homely and comfortable. On North Uist try **Langass Lodge** (tel: 01876 580285) and on South Uist the recently modernised **Lochboisdale Hotel** (tel: 01878 700332).

THE FAR NORTH

The far north of mainland Scotland is so thinly populated that it is possible to set out with a backpack and walk for several days and see hardly another living soul. In contrast to the dramatic Atlantic coast, with its long sea lochs, the eastern coasts this far north are lined by a broad strip of lowland which broadens out into the spacious windswept plain of Caithness. This, and the important 19th-century herring industry, accounts for the much greater density of settlement on the east coast and the more worldly atmosphere than in the west.

The Orkney and Shetland islands have a completely different cultural atmosphere from the rest of Scotland. They were Norse dominions from 875 to 1468, and indeed have always been exposed to foreign influences more than any other region of the British Isles. The islands have spectacular cliff scenery and huge seabird colonies, making them key destinations for birdwatchers.

Wool for sale on Harris, where knitted socks and jerseys are a real cottage industry

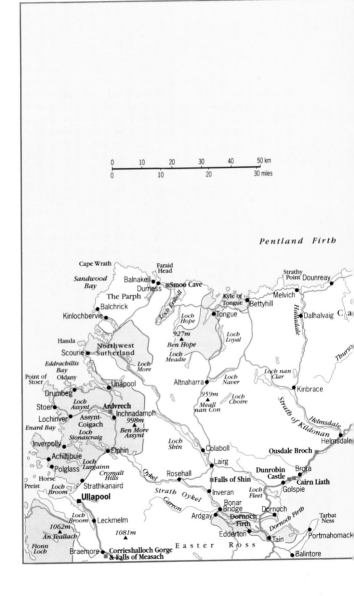

THE FAR NORTH MAP

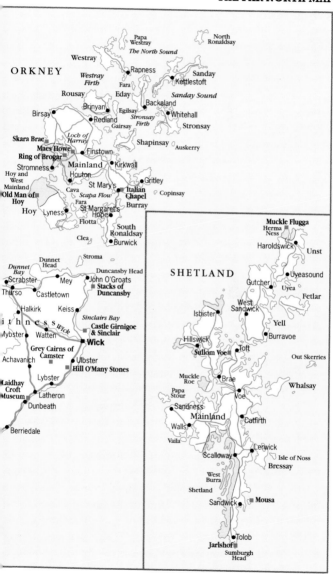

THE MAINLAND: CAITHNESS AND SUTHERLAND

CAPE WRATH

From the Kyle of Durness, take a ferry and minibus to view the extraordinary coastal scenery at mainland Britain's northwesterly tip, battered by the sea. The wild headland's 300-foot (90m) cliffs echo with the screams of seabirds.

DORNOCH

A quiet and pretty seaside resort with miles of sandy beaches, Dornoch has a small restored 13th-century cathedral, but is most famous for its splendid golf links. By the 17th hole is a stone commemorating the last witch to be burned in the country, in 1722.

DUNROBIN CASTLE

11 miles (17km) northeast of Dornoch

Dunrobin, with its fairytale towers, stands on a natural terrace above the sea. An ancient fortress centred on a medieval keep, it is the seat of the Dukes of Sutherland. The interior contains some excellent pictures.

Open: daily, June to September; weekdays in May.

DURNESS

60 miles (96km) west of John O'Groats

Durness is famous for its beautiful beach, along with that of neighbouring Balnakeil

where dunes hide an old Celtic chapel. The A838 passes close to the path down to the enormous **Smoo cavern**, formed by the joint erosion of the sea and the Alt Smoo Burn.

HILL O'MANY STONES AND GREY CAIRNS OF CAMSTER

10 miles (16km) south of Wick

The **Hill o'Many Stones** is a mysterious fan-shaped arrangement of 22 rows of stones. It is probably later in date than the nearby **Cairns of Camster**, two well-restored neolithic burial cairns. You can crawl through the passage to the chambers if you are so inclined.

JOHN O'GROATS AND THE STACKS OF DUNCANSBY

Not, in fact, the northern tip of mainland Britain (which is Dunnet Head to the west), John O'Groats is named after the Dutchman Jan de Groot, who settled there in the 16th century. The place itself is a major disappointment, but if you carry on to **Duncansby Head** you will find a truly exhilarating landscape, with the three great pillars of Duncansby Stacks clinging to the cliffs.

THURSO

20 miles (32km) west of John O'Groats

A former fishing village and quarry town, Thurso has a castle overlooking the old harbour, and an absorbing little **folk museum** whose star exhibit is the Ulbster stone with its

*Duncansby Stacks – guardians of
the edge of the world*

intriguing Pictish symbols.
Bang in the 20th century is the
nearby **Dounreay nuclear
reactor** (daily tours in summer).

TONGUE
The village is splendidly sited
on the north coast, overlooking
the long reach of Kyle of Tongue,
on whose shores can be seen
the ruins of the 14th-century
Mackay look-out post. The more
comfortable-looking **Tongue
House** was built by the Mackay
chiefs in more secure days.

WICK
The busy town of Wick was
once the centre of the herring
industry in the British Isles, and
its harbour had been important
long before that (the name is
from Norse for 'bay'). Visit the
town **Heritage Centre** at Bank
Row (local history) and the
three **castles**: 12th-century Old
Wick, 15th-century Girnigoe
and 17th-century Sinclair.

ORKNEY ISLANDS
The 70 or so Orkney Islands lie
north of the mainland across the
Pentland Firth. Generally flat
and treeless, they are visited in
the main for their rich
prehistoric remains.

KIRKWALL
Mainland Island
This pretty town is the obvious
base for a tour. The great
Cathedral of St Magnus here
was founded in the 12th century.
In one of the massive pillars of
this time, two skeletons were
discovered, one of which may
be of St Magnus himself. In the
precincts are the ruins of the
Bishop's and Earl's palaces, and
nearby **Tankerness House**, a
16th-century town house used
as a museum of the Orkneys.
Open: cathedral: weekdays;
precincts open only in summer;
house: daily, May to September.

◆◆◆
MAES HOWE
Mainland Island

The largest and best preserved chambered cairn in Europe was built around 2700 BC (at least a century before Stonehenge in Wiltshire). A 40-foot (12m) tunnel beneath a great mound of earth (Maes Howe means 'great mound') leads to a large chamber with three burial cells opening off it. The bones of those buried there remained undisturbed for 2,000 years until the tomb was looted by Vikings, who left runic inscriptions on the walls (still visible).
Open: daily.
Closed: Wednesday and Thursday mornings in winter.

The Old Man of Hoy is a 'novelty' scramble for rock climbers

◆◆
OLD MAN OF HOY
Mainland Island

Hoy, off the southwest corner of Mainland, is Orkney's only dramatic island. The famous Old Man of Hoy is a huge stack rearing 450 feet (135m) out of the sea, sometimes visible from the Caithness coast. Try to see it, and the 1,140-foot (347m) St John's Head, from the Stromness ferry.

◆◆
RING OF BROGAR
Mainland Island

This great circle, originally consisting of 60 stones, was surely one of the most magnificent stone circles erected by neolithic man. Though only 20 or so stones remain, the effect is still breathtaking.

◆◆◆ SKARA BRAE

Mainland Island
This is one of the most
fascinating ancient sites of
Western Europe, a complete
neolithic settlement that lay
perfectly preserved in sand
dunes for 4,000 years until
uncovered by a storm in 1850.
It is not only the extent or the
age but the beauty and
ingenuity of the buildings and
the thoughtfulness of the
domestic arrangements that
move and amaze.
A ground plan of the settlement
looks like a microscopic
organism divided into cells and
linked by a tight web of
passages and channels. The
houses are furnished with beds,
dressers, cupboards – all made
of stone. The inhabitants' pots,
jewellery, clothes and tools are
displayed in the museum. A
community of something like
50 people lived here, and the
site was occupied for around
600 years.
Open: daily.

◆ STROMNESS

Mainland Island
Once an important port,
Stromness is now simply a
delightful harbour town with fine
crowstepped houses along its
steep winding streets. The **Pier
Arts Centre** (*open*: Tuesday to
Saturday) has the best collection
of modern British art in the north
of Scotland, including
masterpieces by Ben Nicholson
and Barbara Hepworth –
strangely complementary to the
islands' ancient remains.

SHETLAND

Going some 60 miles (95km)
north from Orkney, you come
to the Shetland Islands, bleak
inland but with dramatic
shorelines. The 'simmer dim' –
midsummer nights when
darkness never quite descends
because of the northerly
latitude – is something of
unbelievable beauty.

◆ HERMA NESS AND MUCKLE FLUGGA

Unst
The point at Herma Ness is the
northernmost part of the British
Isles. It is a nature reserve
famous for its colony of great
skuas and puffins. Beyond the
dramatic cliffs lies the island of
Muckle Flugga – looking like
the back of some prehistoric
monster – with its lighthouse.

◆◆ JARLSHOF

Mainland Island
At the southern end of Shetland,
near Sumburgh airport, is one
of the prime archaeological
sites in Scotland, continuously
inhabited from the Bronze Age
right up until the 17th century.
There are remains of Bronze
Age houses built round
courtyards, Iron Age wheel-
houses, Viking longhouses, a
medieval farmstead and the
16th- and 17th-century houses
of Stewart earls.
Open: April to September.
Closed: Sunday mornings.

◆ LERWICK

This is the main town and
capital of Shetland, and the

Remains of the Broch of Clickhimin

centre of the fishing industry. The development of Europe's largest oil terminal at **Sullom Voe** (35 miles/56km north) ha given the town a new lease of life in recent decades. In the southern, older, part of the town are narrow lanes and little 'lodeberries' – enclosed spaces behind houses. The 17th-century **Fort Charlotte** overlooking the Sound of Bressay, the **Broch of Clickhimin**, and an interesting museum of Shetland are some of the town's attractions.

◆◆◆
MOUSA BROCH ✓

12 miles (20km) south of Lerwick on Mousa Island
On a little island off Mainland, on a headland, the best preserved broch in Scotland still stands over 36 feet (12m) tall, probably not much below its original height. Of the typical features of these Iron Age towers, the most fascinating to be preserved here is the staircase which leads to the top within the double outer wall. *Open*: at all times but only accessible by 15-minute boat ride from Sandwick jetty.

ACCOMMODATION AND EATING OUT

Caithness and Sutherland
Ben Loyal (tel: 01847 611216) is a small, friendly hotel in Tongue. The **Summer Isles Hotel**, Achiltibuie, North of Ullapool (tel: 01854 622282) is comfortable, with excellent food.
Orkney
Merkister Hotel, Harray, Orkney (tel: 01856 771366) is economical and pleasant. The homely **Ayre Hotel** (tel: 01856 873001) is well established on the Kirkwall shore. Grander and more isolated is **Balfour Castle**, Shapinsay (tel: 01856 711282). Don't miss the award-winning **Creel Inn and Restaurant**, at St Magaret's Hope.
Shetland
The **Shetland Hotel**, Holmsgarth Road, Lerwick (tel: 01595 695515) is a large, comfortable, modern hotel. **Busta House Hotel**, Busta (tel: 01806 522506) has an excellent bar and restaurant. **Burrastow House** (tel: 01595 809307) with only three rooms, overlooks a bay with otters.

Peace and Quiet

Wildlife and Countryside in Scotland by Paul Sterry

Scotland can boast some of the most beautiful and rugged scenery in the whole of the British Isles: dramatic mountain peaks, deep lochs and glens, vast tracts of open moorland and windswept, rocky coasts are among the many outstanding features. With outdoor pursuits featuring strongly among the activities of visitors to the region, the natural history of Scotland can be enjoyed to the full.

The Scottish Highlands are what most visitors perceive as the quintessential Scottish landscape. Much of central and northwest mainland Scotland is dominated by upland terrain, home to red deer, golden eagles and mountain hares. Mountain flowers also flourish on many mountain tops, although the prevailing acid bedrock and overgrazing by sheep have certainly not favoured great diversity. Lochs and lochans are also a notable feature of the upland landscape, adding not only beauty, but also natural history interest to the terrain. The third feature of the uplands (and indeed of many lowland areas

of Scotland) is forest. The great Caledonian forest that once cloaked much of the land has all but disappeared, but sizeable tracts of pine and birch forest can still be found in certain areas and these support a rich variety of animals and plants. Then there is the coastline. Cliffs and islands, particularly on the west and north coasts have huge colonies of seabirds. The Scottish islands themselves are varied and distinct. Each has a unique charm and many are 'musts' for visiting naturalists. In the text, RSPB is short for the Royal Society for the Protection of Birds. The following places are listed alphabetically, not by region.

Ailsa Craig
offshore island accessible from Girvan. Contact the Girvan Tourist Information Centre for details
Ailsa Craig is famous, in particular, for its large gannetry which numbers more than 20,000 nests. Other sea birds, including puffins, razorbills and kittiwakes also nest here and boat trips usually allow several hours to view the birds.

PEACE AND QUIET

Monarch of the Glen

Full grown red deer stags are a magnificent sight and deserve the description 'Monarch of the Glen'. In the autumn, males gather for the rut and joust for the right to mate with the females – called hinds. Loud bellowing sounds and the clash of antlers are a familiar sound on crisp October mornings on the Scottish moors. In the summer months, the red deer herds tend to live higher up the hills than in winter. They are generally rather wary of man, and justifiably so because they are hunted by stalkers with high-powered rifles.

Bass Rock

island in the Firth of Forth, accessible by boat from North Berwick during the summer months. Contact the boatman, Fred Marr (tel: 01620 892838) for details of sailings

Often inaccessible because of rough seas, the Bass Rock offers a spectacular setting for more than 20,000 nesting pairs of gannets. Many birds nest within a few feet of the path to the lighthouse, giving excellent views to visitors.

Fred Marr also occasionally lands visitors on nearby **Craigleith**, a small island which offers excellent views of a wide variety of breeding seabirds. A visit to this island is only recommended for the serious seabird enthusiast.

Beinn Eighe

National Nature Reserve near Kinlochewe

Dominated by the backdrop of the mountain summits, Britain's first National Nature Reserve was established to protect one of the best remaining areas of Caledonian pine forest. Trails start from the car park at the southern end of Loch Maree on the A832. There is also a visitor centre, open during the summer months only. Red deer are easily seen, but other inhabitants of the pine forests – notably pine martens and wildcats – are more elusive and seldom observed. Birds of Beinn Eighe include golden eagle, Scottish crossbill and ptarmigan; an assortment of arctic-alpine flowers grow at higher elevations.

Cairngorm Plateau

mountain plateau near Aviemore

Although there are numerous hill walking routes that lead to the plateau, probably the best option for visitors to the region is to 'cheat' and use the ski-lift service which takes you to a short distance below Cairngorm summit. Once there, you can set off in almost any direction. However, it is probably best to follow recognised routes, worn bare by armies of walkers. The plateau is a National Nature Reserve and efforts are being made to combat the effects of foot erosion. Please observe any signs relating to conservation measures.

As you walk away from the highly disturbed summit area, there is a good chance of seeing dotterel, ptarmigan or perhaps even a snow bunting. Upland plants are best seen by exploring trails and streams from the ski-lift car park. This same car park often has small flocks of snow buntings during the winter months.

Dunnet Bay
near Castletown in northwest Caithness
Visitors to John O'Groats with an interest in natural history should visit Dunnet Bay and surrounding sites. The bay itself is best viewed either from the southern end at Castletown or from the car park at the caravan site off the A836. From September until April long-tailed ducks and great northern divers are among the attractions.
Nearby **St John's Loch**, next to the A836, harbours geese and ducks during the winter months; in spring and summer, Dunnet Head has breeding seabirds and its flora includes the diminutive Scottish primrose.

Edinburgh
Holyrood Park offers good opportunities for relaxing among natural surroundings amid the capital's bustle. However, more than this, the park has considerable natural history interest. The slopes of Arthur's Seat – a dramatic, rocky outcrop – have a varied flora which includes heathers, bloody cranesbill and purple milk-vetch. In the **Royal Botanic Gardens**, off Inverleith Row, you can see many Scottish native flowers, and woodland birds are also common.

Seabird city – massed gannets on Bass Rock

Fowlsheugh
seabird cliffs near Stonehaven on the east coast. RSPB reserve
The sandstone cliffs here provide numerous ledges for nesting seabirds including kittiwakes, guillemots, fulmars and puffins. To reach the reserve, drive south from Stonehaven on the A92 and turn off to Crawton and park. Best from May until July.

Insh Marshes
RSPB reserve near Kingussie
Parts of this reserve are viewable from the B9152 between Kingussie and Aviemore but the reserve information centre can be reached by taking the B970 from Kingussie towards Drumguish. There are two hides overlooking the marshes

PEACE AND QUIET

for observing geese and ducks, especially during the winter months. Loch Insh itself, viewable from a minor road at its northern end, sometimes has ospreys and Slavonian grebes.

Islay

This delightful island off the west coast of Scotland is best known for its wintering barnacle geese but has many other wildlife and scenic attractions. One of the best places to see the geese – both barnacles and Greenland white-fronts – is around **Loch Gruinart**. Much of the area is an RSPB reserve and visitors must view from the road (B8017) to avoid disturbance. The shores and coastal waters of western Islay are excellent for wintering waders and sea duck and the island is also one of the best places to see choughs – red-billed members of the crow family. They, and many other species of birds, breed around the coast.

The Cairngorms from Loch Insh

Scottish Heather

Heather is not unique to Scotland. However, this low-growing, hardy plant does find the moors of Scotland particularly to its liking and puts on a spectacular flowering show in July and August. The true name of heather is ling, *Calluna vulgaris*, and its pink flowers are seen in a whole range of shades, some almost white. Other species of heathers also grow on Scottish moorland but ling is by far the commonest and the only one to carpet whole hillsides. The shoots of ling are a favourite food of grouse, as well as several caterpillars, including that of the emperor moth, a bright green and black creature.

Inverpolly

National Nature Reserve near Ullapool. Restricted access during deer stalking season
Inverpolly boasts a mixture of habitats ranging from mountain and moorland to woodland and loch. Several species of

waders, including greenshank, breed on the moorland, and you can find a wide variety of upland flowers. There is an information centre at Knockan on the A835. A few miles further north on the A835 is **Inchnadamph**, another National Nature Reserve, famous for its limestone scenery and associated flora which includes several species of orchids.

Loch Fleet

near Golspie on the east coast of Scotland
Loch Fleet is a large body of tidal water, almost completely surrounded by land. It connects with the sea at Littleferry and at low tide vast areas of mudflats are revealed. Loch Fleet is best viewed either from Littleferry or from the A9 which crosses at the landward end of the Loch. Littleferry can be reached by driving south on the minor road from Golspie that also leads to the golf course.
Loch Fleet is a superb place to watch sea duck and waders feeding. Although there is something to see at any time of year, numbers of birds are greatest in late winter to early spring.
At **Littleferry**, look for large numbers of long-tailed ducks, scoters and eiders. Rarer species, such as surf scoter and king eider, are regularly seen; **Embo**, a few miles down the coast, is another good spot for congregations of sea ducks. Divers, sea ducks and waders can also be seen by walking along the sandy beach between Golspie and Littleferry.
If you are driving between

Loch Mallachie, part of the Loch Garten nature reserve

Golspie and Littleferry during the summer, stop to explore the pine plantations beside the road, where you may find interesting flowers such as serrated wintergreen and lesser twayblade orchid.

Loch Garten

RSPB reserve in the heart of the Abernethy Forest near Aviemore
Best known for its breeding ospreys, this is arguably the most famous wildlife attraction in Scotland. To reach the reserve, turn off the A95 to Boat of Garten and then on to the B970, following signposts to 'Loch Garten' and 'to the Ospreys'.
To see the nesting ospreys, park in the main car park and walk to the observation hide; May to July are the best months. There is plenty of scope for walking through the pines of **Abernethy Forest**. Perhaps the best route is from the car park at the northwest corner of Loch Garten. An easy track leads

PEACE AND QUIET

Twinflower – look for it on moors and in conifer woods

along the edge of the loch to the smaller Loch Mallachie. Among the trees, look for red squirrels, crested tits, capercaillies and Scottish crossbills. Ospreys are sometimes seen fishing on the lochs. The ground flora includes such plants as common wintergreen, lesser twayblade and chickweed wintergreen.

Ospreys are also regular visitors to some of the fish farms in the area, notably ones near Aviemore. For a small fee, the owners sometimes allow birdwatchers to watch the birds fishing; ask at the Information Centre in Aviemore.

Loch Leven

near Kinross close to Junction 6 of the M90

This large body of water, much of which is a National Nature Reserve, is a great spot to observe wildfowl and other water birds. Many species

breed during the summer months but even greater numbers and variety appear during the winter. One of the best places to observe the birds is at the RSPB's **Vane Farm** reserve in the southeast corner of the loch. There is a visitor centre, a walk to a viewpoint and an observation hide. Another viewing point is at **Kirkgate Park** in Kinross itself. Species commonly seen on Loch Leven in the winter months include whooper and Bewick's swans, pink-footed geese, greylag geese and tufted ducks.

Loch Rannoch

open water, moorland and pine forest to the west of Pitlochry

To reach Loch Rannoch, take the B846 west from the A9 and then the minor road which runs along the south of the loch. Look for ducks on the water and common sandpipers and redshank around the edge of the loch.

The **Black Wood of Rannoch**, a remnant area of natural pine forest, lies along the southern shore; there are parking areas beside the road. The forest is home to birds such as capercaillies and Scottish crossbills, and red squirrels. The ground flora includes such specialities as lesser twayblade and chickweed wintergreen.

The minor road ends at Rannoch Station. Park here and walk out across the open heather moorland which supports several species of dragonfly as well as an unusual plant called Rannoch rush.

Mull
*island off western Strathclyde,
easily accessible by ferry from
Oban*
With an intricate coastline,
mountain and moorland,
freshwater and woodland, it is
not surprising that opportunities
for observing wildlife here are
good.
The road that hugs the west
coast of Mull offers an excellent
way of seeing the varied terrain.
Stop from time to time to scan
the shore and open water for
birds such as great northern
divers, black guillemots, gulls
and waders; this is also a likely
area to see otters. The shores of
Loch Na Keal are particularly
rewarding and grey herons can
sometimes be seen at close
range.
Coastal flowers can be found
along the shoreline and several
species of mountain flowers
grow almost at sea-level where
the road passes under the
shadow of **Ben More**.
Mull is one of the few places in
Scotland, or indeed western
Europe, where whales and
dolphins are regularly seen and
where there is an opportunity
for casual visitors to see them.
Contact the **Sealife Centre**,
Quinish, Dervaig, Mull (tel:
01688 400223) for details.
Minke whales are the most
regularly seen species.

Orkney Islands
*by ferry from Scrabster in
Caithness to Stromness*
A varied series of islands, most
of which are accessible either
by ferries or bridges. While
much of the land is fertile and
under agricultural use, there
are also areas of flower-rich
moorland, dramatic sea cliffs
with vast seabird colonies and
numerous freshwater lochs and
pools.
There is an RSPB reserve on
Birsay Moors, near Cottasgarth
on Mainland Island. From
roadside observation hides
moorland birds such as hen
harriers, short-eared owls and
curlews can be seen. Also on
Mainland is another RSPB
reserve at **Marwick Head**; turn
off the B9056 in northwest

Mull, with Duart Castle

PEACE AND QUIET

Charming, clumsy-looking and colourful, puffins are also surprisingly approachable

Scottish Crossbill
The Scottish crossbill is the only bird endemic to Britain (that is to say found nowhere else in the world). It gets its name from the shape of its bill, the two mandibles of which overlap and are used to prise the seeds out from pine cones.
Scottish crossbills are found mainly in remnant areas of Caledonian pine forest such as Abernethy and Rothiemurchus, both in the shadow of the Cairngorms. They nest early in the year, often sitting on eggs while there is still snow on the ground.

Mainland on a minor road, park beyond Marwick and walk to the cliff edge. The dramatic sandstone cliffs provide ledges for thousands of sea birds including fulmars, guillemots, kittiwakes and razorbills. Also look for predatory skuas which feed here but breed inland on the moorland. **Yesnaby Cliffs**, on the west coast of Mainland, can be reached by turning off the B9056 just after it splits with the A967. The cliffs themselves are dramatic, and the short turf harbours a good population of the diminutive and rare Scottish primrose.
The island of **Hoy** can be reached by ferry from Stromness and is most famous for the Old Man of Hoy, an offshore stack. The awesome

St John's Cliffs near by are full of seabirds from May until July. Great and arctic skuas breed on the moorland and the plantlife includes dwarf willow, bearberry and alpine bearberry. Around the coast you should see red-throated divers and skuas while peregrines and golden eagles can be seen with luck almost anywhere away from habitation.

Rothiemurchus Forest
extensive pine forest near Aviemore in the Highlands
Rothiemurchus Forest is an extensive area of pine woodland, much of it mature plantation, but with small relict patches of native forest. Lochs and open moorland add to the interest of the area. There is a visitor centre at Inverdruie, near Aviemore and a signposted car park at Loch an Eilein. Look for moorland flowers, and red squirrels and Scottish crossbills in the trees.

St Abb's Head
dramatic coastal walk near Eyemouth in the Borders
Park at the signposted car park at Northfield Farm, just before St Abbs. A cliff-top walk leads to the headland which harbours breeding sea birds in abundance; look for guillemots and kittiwakes in particular.

Shetland Isles
Mainland Island can be reached by car ferry from Aberdeen or by scheduled flights from London and Aberdeen. Regular car ferries link most of the Shetland Isles, and the road networks are surprisingly good for such remote islands. They have some of the most dramatic coastal scenery in western Europe, hosting huge seabird colonies. Open moorland, freshwater lochs and farmland comprise much of the interior. At the southernmost tip of Mainland lies **Sumburgh Head** where seabirds are plentiful. If driving south from Lerwick, stop off at the **Pool of Virkie**, near the airport, to look for waders and wildfowl. Off the east coast of Mainland lies the small island of **Mousa**, famous for its Pictish broch (see page 92). Seals are plentiful on the shores and coastal birds, including black guillemots, can be seen. European storm petrels actually nest in wall cavities in the broch itself.
The **Isle of Noss** off Bressay is a National Nature Reserve lying off the east coast of Bressay. There is a ferry to the island during calm weather every day except Mondays and Thursdays during the summer months. This is perhaps the best location on Shetland for seabirds if your visit is a short one. A circular tour of the island will enable you to see most of Shetland's seabird species, many at incredibly close range. **Herma Ness** is another National Nature Reserve at the northern tip of Unst. There is roadside parking at the southern end of Burra Firth and from there visitors walk to the cliffs. Large numbers of skuas breed on the moorland and the cliffs have gannets, kittiwakes, guillemots and many more. Inhabitants of the large puffin colonies often surprise human visitors by their indifference to their presence.

PEACE AND QUIET

Seascape and Scolpaig Tower on North Uist

Fetlar can be reached by ferries from North Yell and Unst. The RSPB manages a large part of the island and there is restricted access during the breeding season. Skuas and whimbrel are among the attractions of Fetlar and there is often a resident snowy owl. Red-necked phalaropes can sometimes be spotted on pools beside the road and otters are often seen around the coast. For more information, ask at the RSPB warden's cottage on the island.

Solway Firth

The Solway is an important area for wintering ducks, geese, swans and waders. The best locations for observing the birds are at **Caerlaverock National Nature Reserve** and the **Wildfowl Trust Refuge**. There is no access to the NNR itself but good views can be had from the roadside car park on the B725 near Caerlaverock Castle. The refuge is reached by taking the signposted road off the B725 north of the castle. Barnacle geese and whooper swans are specialities here.

The Western Isles

reached by ferry from mainland
For the naturalist, North and South Uists offer the best opportunities for observing wildlife on a short visit. There are still remnant areas of the flower-rich grassland, known as 'machair', that once covered most of the western half of the islands; explore minor roads heading west from the A865 on **South Uist**. Waders are abundant in undisturbed areas and this is one of the last refuges for the endangered corncrake, whose rasping call can be heard all night long in some meadows. **Loch Druidibeg National Nature Reserve**, also on South Uist, can be viewed from the B890 and is a haven for greylag geese. On **North Uist**, be sure to visit the RSPB's reserve at Balranald, which is signposted off the A865 in the northwest of the island. A haven for corncrakes, Balranald has some excellent areas of machair, full of flowers, and a host of breeding birds.

Practical

This section includes information on food, drink, shopping, accommodation, nightlife, tight budget, special events etc.

FOOD AND DRINK

No-one has ever described Scottish cuisine as exotic or even particularly imaginative, but with a resurgence of interest in healthy, natural foodstuffs, there is now a scattering of highly esteemed restaurants across the country, cooking grouse, venison, river salmon and the best seafood in Europe.

It is not always possible to find interesting food, especially in more out-of-the-way places, but all main centres provide somewhere where the food is hot and filling and, when complemented by a delicious glass of malt whisky, will protect you against the bracing weather.

Scots Specialities

Potatoes and oats are ingredients with a particular Scottish flavour. They are used in many ways in dishes that are filling and nutritious.

The most famous oats dish, and one that is always on offer on Scottish hotel breakfast menus, is porridge. Two other Scottish

---

Haggis

This most Scottish of dishes tastes much better than any description would lead you to believe. Traditionally the dish is made from the heart, lung and liver of a sheep or calf. The meat is chopped with suet, onions, oatmeal and spices, stuffed like a large round sausage into a sheep's gut and boiled. This filling dish is served with 'bashed neeps and tatties' (mashed turnip and potato).

A champion haggis-maker. Haggis recipes can be mild or very spicy

FOOD AND DRINK

culinary specialities are soups and plain baking. Cock-a-leekie soup is one of the traditional recipes still regularly found on Scottish menus, a chicken broth with leeks. Scotch broth is a thick peppery soup with lots of vegetables, based on a hearty meat stock. Scones, Scotch pancakes, shortbread, oatcakes and fruit cake, though simple enough in the making, are delicious; available in tins, shortbread and Dundee cake are worldwide favourites.

Meat and Fish
While roast lamb or thick Aberdeen Angus fillet steaks are available throughout the year, game, such as grouse, pheasant and venison, will be frozen if not in season. Roast grouse is much better fresh (after 12 August – the Glorious Twelfth). Wild duck and pheasant should be on menus after 1 October.
The growth in importance of fish farming to the Scottish

Whisky is matured in oak barrels for anything up to 20 years before bottling

economy means that salmon and trout are now a regular part of the Scottish diet. The waters off Scotland are the cleanest in Europe, so this is an excellent place to eat seafood: the lobsters are some of the best in the world and oysters and mussels are also plentiful. Try traditional Musselburgh pie (beefsteak and oysters) and mussel stew. Vegetarians are not well catered for outside the major cities.

When and Where to Eat
Restaurants in major towns and cities have fairly flexible times for eating, while in small towns and villages timing is rigid. Usual restaurant hours are between 11.00 and 14.30hrs for lunch and 18.00hrs to midnight for dinner. Some places serve a substantial high tea in the early evening (ideal for children).

FOOD AND DRINK

Look out for the blue and white 'Taste of Scotland' symbol on restaurants. This is a scheme, supported by the Scottish Tourist Board, that seeks to promote good food. Each year a book called *A Taste of Scotland* gives details of the best places to eat.

Whisky

The hundreds of different whiskies made in Scotland are traditionally considered the best in the world, thanks to a combination of age-old know-how and the all-important peaty water. They constitute the majority of whisky sales world-wide, and are produced in some 110 distilleries across the country.

With a name derived from the Gaelic *uisge beatha*, meaning the water of life, it is obvious that this caramel coloured spirit has long been taken seriously. It is made with barley, both malted and not, water and yeast, and after two distillations is aged in oak casks for a minimum of three years. With the rapid development of whisky production in the late 19th century came the tradition of 'blending' different distillations to produce a consistent product. Popular international brands such as Bells and Famous Grouse fall into this category.

Recently there has been a resurgence of interest in the traditional 'malt' whiskies whose qualities are defined by the exact barley type and malted strength, and the particulars of the local water supply to the distillery. The final result is then matured for anything from 8 to 20 years. Recommending a particular malt is difficult because everybody has their own favourite, but some of the most popular are Glenfiddich, Glenmorangie, Glenlivet, Macallan and Laphroaig. Scotland also produces a whisky liqueur, Drambuie, which is thick and sweet.

Beer and Pubs

The Scots also have a tradition of brewing fine ale similar in character to English 'bitter' but the Scots varieties often have a sweeter taste and more body. Scots never call it bitter, however, but usually use the brand name or the generic term 'heavy'. Lagers and imported beers are widely available. Licensing laws are flexible with many pubs, open from 11.00 to 23.00hrs. In contrast Sunday licensing hours stick strictly to 12.00 to 14.30hrs and 18.30 to 23.00hrs. In the strictly presbyterian North West they will not open at all.

The Whisky Trail

There is a malt whisky trail in Speyside, Grampian, where many of the most famous distilleries are to be found (though there are also fine ones elsewhere in the Highlands and on the islands of Orkney, Skye, Jura and Islay). The trail takes in nine distilleries, each with a guided tour. If you only have time for one, then Glenlivet (tel: 01542 783200) is a good choice. It is located on the B9008 north of Tomintoul, open mid-March to late October, Monday to Saturday.

SHOPPING

There is a whole range of goods which seem to be synonymous with Scotland – whisky, tartan and shortbread being only the most obvious. Often the best bargains are to be found off the beaten track in more isolated areas. Ask the people about local industries and crafts; they are likely to be friendly and willing to suggest how you can support their local micro-economy.

Tweed, Wool and Tartan

The soft muted colours of traditional tweed cloth go back to pre-Victorian days, when crofters used to spin, dye and weave their sheep's wool into bolts of cloth, the colours of which reflected the dyes that occurred naturally in the mosses, molluscs and earth around them. The industrial revolution in the south had seen the birth of vast woollen mills, while in the Highlands and remote Scottish islands women and men were still spinning and weaving in their homes. The place where this tradition is still in action is the island of Harris, where for a bolt to be labelled genuine Harris Tweed, it must be woven at home. The wool is now dyed with chemicals, which produce more vibrant and longer lasting colours, and distribution is such that an impressive array of tweeds is obtainable all over Scotland. In Brora, Lochcarron and Beauly a finer Scottish tweed can be bought, made from Shetland wool.

As for knitted woollens, no self-respecting medium-sized town is complete without at least one woollen mill, selling everything from Pringle cashmere to thick oiled Shetland sweaters. Such establishments will also sell a range of tartan, or plaid, items such as ties, and sometimes trousers and kilts.

Glass

The Scots are impressive glass-blowers. **Caithness Glass**, perhaps the most famous manufacturer, has factories in Perth, Oban and Wick. The range of goods for sale is vast, and all three offer fascinating tours which include a demonstration of glass-blowing. **Edinburgh Crystal** in Penicuik is another notable centre.

Highland Souvenirs

Among the more unusual of the Highland crafts is antler carving. Because of the large deer population, and the fact that the deer shed their antlers

---

'Clan' Tartans

The tradition of clan tartans, whereby a particular pattern is worn by one extended family, is thought quintessentially Scottish, but was in fact invented by a cunning pair of Lancashire mill-owners in the early 19th century. They took a sample book full of traditional tartans around the landowners of Scotland. In the comfort of their sitting rooms the great ladies of the land mulled over the various plaids before selecting one, which was then named after them – presumably in return for a large order. More recently football clubs and others have created new tartans!

Each kilt uses up to 26 feet (8m) of tartan

every year, a whole series of traditional and ritual Scottish artefacts have come to be carved from the beasts' antlers. If you catch the Scots' bug badly, there is nothing to stop you buying full Highland dress – kilt, bagpipes and all.

Food and Drink

It is well worth taking home some malt whisky once you have found the one that suits your palate, though it is still not exactly cheap even in its native land. Delicious smoked salmon is also widely available; **Letterfinlay's Larder**, Spean Bridge (tel: 01397 712626) will supply it by mail order. If you have developed a taste for haggis, it will survive without refrigeration for a while if your journey home is short. Otherwise, stock up on Scottish pure heather honey, shortbread biscuits and oatcakes in tins.

ACCOMMODATION

Tourism has long been a vital constituent of the Scottish economy, and consequently there are hotels from luxury to basic, hordes of bed and breakfast possibilities and ubiquitous camping and caravan parks. There are many groups of self-catering cabins to rent in locations looking out over breathtaking landscapes. Some of the best hotels are converted castles, shooting lodges and mansions. These add a real sense of historic Scottish luxury to your trip, and will often offer a variety of activities like fishing, stalking, skiing, shooting and golf to their guests. The Scottish Tourist Board can supply information on all types of accommodation.

Bed and Breakfast

The bed and breakfast accommodation (B & B) in Scotland is in a class of its own. Essentially this is just a room in someone's home with a hearty cooked breakfast in the morning. Staying in a B & B is a way of getting to talk to the local people, and is reasonably cheap.

Self-catering

Self-catering accommodation is becoming ever more popular, ranging from flats in the city to cottages and cabins or remote houses. The Scottish Tourist Board publishes a booklet, *Scotland Self-catering* , which lists over 2,000 places for the independent traveller.

For a more unusual selection of self-catering places, contact:

• **National Trust for Scotland**, 5 Charlotte Square, Edinburgh EH2 4DU (tel: 0131 226 5922).

• **Landmark Trust**, Shottesbrooke, Maidenhead, Berks (tel: 01628 825925).

CULTURE, ENTERTAINMENT AND NIGHTLIFE

If you are looking for sophisticated evening entertainment, you will only find it in Glasgow and Edinburgh. Glasgow has become one of the most fashionable cities in Britain, and to complement its daytime designer shops and classy delicatessens, its restaurants, concert halls and theatres, there are scores of live music bars, wine bars, nightclubs and discos.

Festivals

The Glasgow arts festival 'Mayfest' runs for the first three weeks in May. Since its

Luxurious ambience in the Culloden House Hotel, Inverness

inception in 1981 and Glasgow's turn as European capital of culture in 1991, it has grown into an extremely prestigious showcase event, attracting major names in drama, music, ballet, opera and art. However, it is Edinburgh which hosts the largest arts festival in the world. Annually, for three weeks in August, over 1,000 shows are staged throughout the city, not to mention the hectic impromptu street performances which see would-be opera singers busking beside fire-eaters and clowns. Be warned that it is virtually impossible to find anywhere to stay at short notice. You should book as far in advance as you can, and expect to find it pricey.

Small-town Entertainment

Outside these metropolises, nightlife is much less exotic, though Scotland has excellent local discothèques. Otherwise, social life centres on the pub, where a quiet evening drink can turn into a major singsong with bagpipes and melodious, melancholy Gaelic ballads. Traditional dancing parties are called *ceilidhs* (from the Gaelic word for 'visit', and pronounced 'kayley'). They mainly take place in rural hotels and pubs and are advertised locally on posters. A local band will play foot-tapping folk music with the aid of a fiddle and an accordion, and those in the know will swirl confidently through the set steps of a succession of Scottish reels.

WEATHER AND WHEN TO GO

By far the best months to visit Scotland are May and June, when skies can be cloudless, the air windless and the sun hot. Around the summer solstice in the north, dawn begins at 01.00hrs, about an hour after dusk has ended, and with 20 hours of daylight you can pack that much more into your holiday. In July the midges

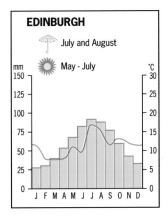

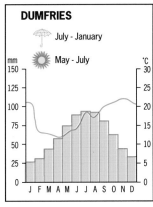

WEATHER AND WHEN TO GO

Shopping for pottery

rainfall. However, the east coast is known for its chill winds from the Siberian steppes.

The winter months are very cold, with strong winds (often gales) and snow is a certainty in the Highlands. Of course, if you want to ski this is obviously the time to go. Apart from the disadvantage of the weather, in winter the daylight hours in Scotland are very short.

What to Wear

Never go to Scotland expecting it to be warm. Edinburgh is, after all, on the same latitude as Moscow. The most essential article of clothing is a waterproof top. You should always have it to hand, as rain sometimes manages to fall from almost clear skies. Rare is the day when you feel comfortable without some kind of woolly (and Scotland is the ideal place to buy one if you are feeling chilly).

For walking, a good pair of boots is vital, as the heather and acidic peat bogs make mincemeat of anything but the stoutest footwear. Many walkers and holiday-makers also carry waterproof over-trousers. Very summery clothes are of limited use, except perhaps a swimming costume. The Scottish waters are always cold, but if the sun is shining you may be tempted to dash into the sea from one of the stunning beaches.

As for evening wear, the Scots are casual dressers, and only in the very smartest hotels do managers insist on formal wear.

which plague much of Scotland begin to bite, and by August, though it can be beautiful, a combination of mosquitoes and unpredictable showers can dampen the holiday spirit. In spring and autumn, weather in the Highlands is totally unpredictable and can change in seconds, from blissful sunshine to cold wind and rain. It is also worth bearing in mind that the west coast can receive almost double the rainfall of the east. In a bad year the west coast town of Fort William might see nearly 10 feet (3m) of

HOW TO BE A LOCAL

Scotland is constantly inundated with long-lost sons and daughters, back in their homeland to trace their ancestors. Present-day natives are proud of their culture and heritage and enjoy sharing their knowledge, but do not be too forthright with your own. Generally, the Scots are friendly and generous people, but there are pockets of deep conservatism, and an over-friendly approach might be viewed with suspicion. This could be particularly true in remote, rural communities. In some parts of Scotland Gaelic, not English, was the first language of the older generation, and you'll do well to appreciate that. Accents also differ very widely, from the 'refinement' of Edinburgh to the inpenetrability of Clydeside.

If you walk down Princes Street dressed in a kilt, a sporran, knitted hose, leather brogues and a tartan beret while carrying a set of bagpipes, you will stick out like an oak tree on a palm-fringed beach. Keep the kilt for Highland games, weddings and *ceilidhs*. The Scots are as keen as any other Europeans on Italian designer clothes, and the young would not be seen dead in a kilt on the street. Those who are forced into tartan do so largely for the benefit of tourists. Lastly, do *not* call any Scot 'Jimmy' – he won't think it's a bit funny. To placate him, offer to buy 'a pint of heavy' or a 'dram' in the nearest pub.

CHILDREN

Although Scotland has long been heavily reliant on tourism, the industry has not felt the need to invest in specially designed entertainment centres for children. This must be because what the country already has to offer provides plenty of fun for most age groups – in spite of the weather. But parents have to be prepared to use plenty of imagination and energy. Scottish beaches are some of the most beautiful in the British Isles, with the sandy west coast beaches perfect for sandcastles. Older children might like to attempt a little surfing (see page 116). In addition there are watersports centres on many of Scotland's lochs, where kids can be taught sailing, waterskiing and even parascending. The same places often offer pony trekking. Highland games are designed as all-round family entertainment, and often include barbecues and stalls as well as competitions for tossing the caber and throwing the hammer. In the background will be bagpipes accompanying displays of Highland dancing. Scotland is a land of tales and legends, and it is not difficult to fire a child's imagination with these. Try a trip to Loch Ness to spot the monster or look for the disappearing village of Brigadoon. The wildlife is another aspect of Scotland to thrill children. At Shin Falls, just north of Lairg in Sutherland, if you go at spawning time your children can watch the salmon leaping up the falls to lay their eggs upstream. The Salmon Ladder near Pitlochry is another such site.

Most hotels, B & Bs and public houses welcome children. In pubs children under 16 must be accompanied by an adult and of course can only consume non-alcoholic drinks. Edinburgh District Council has published a free booklet, *Child Friendly Edinburgh*, which lists pubs and restaurants, shops, leisure facilities and other places where children are welcome.

TIGHT BUDGET

Accommodation
There are lots of budget travellers in Scotland and a plethora of cheap campsites to service them. In addition there are about 80 youth hostels ranging in location from city centre to the remotest glens. For full details contact the **Scottish Youth Hostelling Association**, 7 Glebe Crescent, Stirling, Scotland FK8 2JA (tel: 01786 451181). For the occasional touch of luxury a room in a bed and breakfast will not set you back too much.

Eating Out and Entertainment
Every Scottish town has its fish and chip shop, and often cheap Indian and Chinese restaurants. Pubs in Scotland are an institution of friendliness, and for the price of a couple of pints you can spend an entire evening at the local bar listening to folk music or chatting to the Scots, who are legendary good company.

Shopping
It's a sad fact that shopping in supermarkets is nearly always cheaper than in 'corner' shops. This is particularly the case with alcohol. If you're after food, then go to street markets where, especially late in the day, you can pick up amazing bargains. For rugged clothes, find the local agricultural supplier or government surplus store.

In Brief
● Travel out of season.
● Make sure you have a Youth Hostel Card.
● Look out for B & B rooms in private houses.
● Use the cheap public transport particularly the buses.

SPECIAL EVENTS

Twice a year the Scottish Tourist Board publishes a booklet called *Events in Scotland*. To receive a free copy write to The Scottish Tourist Board, 23 Ravelston Terrace, Edinburgh EH4 3EU. The following list gives the main annual events.

January
Kirkwall (Orkney): the Ba' Games – mass street football (1 January).
Countrywide: Burns' Night, in memory of Scotland's great poet Robert Burns. At traditional gatherings the haggis is 'addressed' with poetry before it is eaten.

And now, ladies and gentlemen…

March
Tobermory (Mull): Drama Festival.
Edinburgh: Folk Festival.
April
Edinburgh: Scottish Royal Academy annual exhibitions.
Hamilton: Hamilton Races (flat).
St Andrews: Kate Kennedy procession – historic university pageant.
May
Glasgow: Mayfest.
June
Hawick: Common Riding, an historic patrolling of parish boundaries, one of a series in the Borders (see page 39).
Kirkwall (Orkney): St Magnus' Festival of Arts and Music.

SPECIAL EVENTS

Isle of Skye: Skye Week.
Edinburgh: Royal Highland Show held at Ingliston Showground, 7 miles (11km) from the city centre (by the airport).
Peebles: Beltane Festival, traditional observance of midsummer solstice, of pagan origin.
July
Glasgow: Folk Festival.
Kelso: Gala Week. Also Border Union Show, large exhibition and horse-racing.
August
Various centres (in rotation): National Sheepdog Trials.
Muir of Ord: Black Isle Agricultural Show.
St Andrews: Lammas Fair (medieval market).
Glasgow: World Pipe Band Championships.

Throwing the hammer

Edinburgh: International Festival of the Arts.
September
Fort William: mountain race, Ben Nevis.
Leuchars: Military and Civil Air Show.
October
Oban: Highland Cattle Autumn Show.
Perth: Aberdeen Angus autumn bull sales and cattle show.
November
Edinburgh: Winter Antiques Fair.
December
Comrie (Tayside): Flambeaux Procession (traditional torchlight parade – 31 December).

Highland Games
No mention of these riotous, day-long traditional Scottish fair-cum-shows has been made in the above list of special events. They take place between June and September, usually on Saturdays, and range from local affairs on the beaches of the Outer Hebrides to massive gatherings, such as Braemar. The following list gives the locations of the principal games.
June
Aberdeen, Grantown-on-Spey.
July
Dufftown, Dundee, Elgin, Forres, Kenmore, Inveraray, Inverness, Lochaber (Fort William), Lochearnhead, Dingwall.
August
Mallaig, Aberfeldy, Glasgow, Perth, Crieff, Oban, Dunoon, Birnam, Strathpeffer, Aboyne, Rothesay (Bute), Portree.
September
Braemar, Pitlochry.

SPORT

Scotland has an extraordinary variety of outdoor activity sports. It has long boasted that golf was invented here, and certainly Scotland has some of the best golf courses in the world. Scottish salmon and sea-trout fishing is also world famous, and the bountiful sea provides further opportunities to the fisherman. If you are fond of walking and nature, the north of Scotland is one of the last great wildernesses in Europe, with only golden eagles and red deer to interrupt your solitary ramble. In addition to all this there is pony-trekking, skiing, sailing, waterskiing and even surfing.

Fishing

Sea fishing is readily and reasonably available from hundreds of harbours; simply look out for the signs. Freshwater fishing ranges from exclusive 'beats' on some of the best salmon rivers in the world, to coarse fishing in hundreds of lochs and streams. The nearest Tourist Information Centre will have a leaflet listing the possibilities and how to go about it. The salmon season varies according to the river – some start fishing in January, some in March. For more general information, contact the **Scottish Anglers National Association**, Caledonia House, South Gyle, Edinburgh EH12 9QD (tel: 0131 339 8808).

Golf

There are over 400 golf courses in Scotland, (the so-called 'home of golf'), often nestled behind the dunes of some windswept beach. The most famous ones are exclusive, and it can be very difficult to get a round in midsummer on the Old Course at St Andrews or at Gleneagles. Book as far in advance as you can. These courses are famous for good reason, because the best players in the world test their skills against them. For a little gentle holiday golf, they can be rather demoralising to play on, so do not feel sad if you fail to get on to one. Go and have a better game on one of the many delightful courses elsewhere, and buy yourself a congratulatory drink with the green fee you have saved.

Walking

Two hundred and seventy-nine of Scotland's mountains top the 3,000-foot (914m) mark. They are known as Munros, after Sir Hugh Munro, who collated them into his 'Munro's Tables', and many a 'munro-bagger' has the ambition to scale them all. But this might take you a lifetime! There are three Long Distance Walks in Scotland, established by the Countryside Commission, which can take a whole holiday to complete. Details of the Southern Upland Way (212 miles/341km), the West Highland Way (95 miles/153km) and the Speyside Way (48 miles/77km) are obtainable from Tourist Information Offices. When you go walking always tell someone your route and what time you expect to return. It is vital to go properly prepared for the cold and wet, and also to have maps and a

SPORT

compass should the cloud come right down, as it can. The weather in the hills is very changeable, and claims its victims every year.

Skiing

There are only a few days in the year when the skiing conditions in Scotland are perfect. Either there is not enough snow, or it is too warm and the snow has melted and frozen overnight into sheet ice, or an icy gale causes chair-lifts to swing dangerously and the sun is nowhere to be seen. If you time it right, however, it can be every bit as delightful as skiing anywhere, though the choice of runs is not enormous. Scotland's main resort is Aviemore, in the Cairngorms, but there is also skiing to be had in Glen Coe and Glenshee. Equipment can always be hired.

Surfing

Since the European Amateur Surfing Championships were held in Thurso in 1981, an increasing number of surfers have been braving Scotland's icy waters to follow the wave. The best surfing is in the far north, while the inexperienced surfer will find the sandy-bottomed beaches at Melvich and Sandside more reassuring than Thurso itself or Brimm's Ness.

Sailing and Waterskiing

During the summer, many of Scotland's largest lochs sprout watersport centres from which anyone can hire the equipment to sail, canoe or waterski in the relative calm of the inland waters.

On Bidean nam Bian, Argyll, overlooking Glen Coe

Directory

This section, contains day-to-day information, including travel, health, documentation and language tips.

Contents

Arriving

By Air

Scotland does not have a national airline. There are scheduled flights with various airlines from North America and Europe, and other visitors can fly by way of London. Between them, from London, **British Airways** (tel: 0345 222111) and **British Midland** (tel: 0345 554554) fly direct from Heathrow to Edinburgh, Glasgow, Inverness and Aberdeen. Both airlines offer special Apex (economy) fares, which depend on booking in advance and specifying your dates. From each airport there is a bus service to the city centre as well as taxis. Many of the islands are linked to these airports, and to other local airports, by regular flights (see also page 124). Many European airlines fly direct to Scotland. **British Airways** has a direct service from Düsseldorf, Frankfurt, Milan, Munich and Paris. **Air UK** (tel: 0345 666777) flies from Amsterdam, Bergen, Copenhagen, Oslo and Stavanger.

By Train

British Rail runs frequent services from London to

DIRECTORY

Edinburgh, Glasgow and beyond. There are two main rail routes. One follows the west coast from London Euston station (tel: 0171 387 8541) to Glasgow Central station. The journey on the fast train takes 4 hours 50 minutes. There are excellent sleeper services from Euston to Edinburgh, Glasgow, Aberdeen and Fort William. The east coast service leaves London's King's Cross (tel: 0171 278 2477) for Edinburgh Waverley station. The fastest train takes a little over 4 hours. Book in advance, especially in the holiday season. British Rail offers discounted Apex and Super-Apex fares if you book far enough ahead.

By Bus

There are coach services to Scotland from all over the British Isles, and you can usually choose between day and night-time services. The journey from London takes about 8 hours, and the main London terminal is Victoria Coach Station, though cheaper services often leave from near King's Cross Station. Call National Express (tel: 0990 808080) for details of their Victoria departures, and services from other cities.

By Car

The journey north from London to Edinburgh or Glasgow by motorway takes about 8 hours including stops. The distance is some 450 miles (725km). The quickest route to Scotland is to follow the M1 then join the M6. North of Carlisle, the A74 takes you straight to Glasgow. Fork

right on to the A702 to Edinburgh shortly before Glasgow. It is no longer possible to transport your car to Scotland by train.

Entry Formalities

EU citizens do not need a passport. Citizens of North America need a passport but not a visa. Motorists from abroad with their own cars must carry a green card (insurance) and an international driving licence.

Camping

There is a wide choice of caravan parks, some offering caravans for hire as well as welcoming tourers. Among the firms that rent out campers (motorised caravans) or trailers are **Dumfries Caravan Centre** (Annan Road, Dumfries DG1 3JZ, tel: 01387 252917) and **Sharp's Motorhomes** ('Shangri-la', Culloden Road, Balloch near Inverness IV1 2HQ, tel: 01463 790543). There is also space to pitch a tent in most of the caravan parks. It is possible to camp away from the recognised sites, especially in the remote parts of the Highlands but ask permission should you encounter a local. On the routes of major treks a network of simple unlocked shelters, known as *bothies*, protect hikers from the unpredictable weather.

Car Rental

You should have no difficulty finding car rental firms in any Scottish town. The big international companies are

Camping by Loch na Keal

represented at airports and major railway stations. Elsewhere, look under 'Car Hire' in the Yellow Pages.

Crime

In rural Scotland, it is more likely that someone will drive 50 miles (80km) to return the wallet you left in the pub than that you will be mugged. There is very little to fear in the countryside, and as a visitor you are unlikely to be aware of the poaching that is an accepted part of the Scottish economy. Parts of Scotland's large cities are, inevitably, more dangerous than others, but as a visitor you are unlikely to find yourself in them. Theft from and of cars is endemic in parts of Britain, so always lock up, and never leave valuables inside. If you leave luggage in a parked car keep it out of sight wherever possible.

Disabled Travellers

It is a sad fact of modern British life that a person in a wheelchair has considerable difficulties using public transport. However, increasing numbers of taxis in Scotland can now accommodate wheelchairs (indicated by a wheelchair sign by their 'For Hire' light). To find out about suitable hotels, tours and activities, it is a good idea to enlist the help of an expert travel agency. For full information and a list of travel agents write to **Society for the Advancement of Travel for the Handicapped**, 26 Court Street, Brooklyn, New York, NY 11242. **The Royal Association for Disability and Rehabilitation** (RADAR), 12 City Forum, 250 City Road, London EC1V 8AF (tel: 0171 250 3222) publishes

DIRECTORY

an excellent booklet *Holidays in the British Isles: A guide for disabled people*. In Scotland the most informative centre is **Disability Scotland**, Princes House, 5 Shandwick Place, Edinburgh EH2 4RG (tel: 0131 229 8632). Every year they publish lists and the latest details on hotels, places of interest, transport facilities and other relevant information for the disabled. The Scottish Tourist Board produces a free booklet, *Practical Information for Visitors with Disabilities.*

Driving
Scotland, like the rest of the British Isles, drives on the left. Front-seat passengers are required to wear seat-belts, as are back-seat passengers where belts are provided. Maximum permitted speeds are 70mph (112kph) on motorways, 60mph (96kph) on ordinary roads and 30mph (48kph) in built-up areas except where otherwise indicated. One of the few Scottish idiosyncracies, particularly in the northwest, is the single-track roads, with clearly marked passing places. *Do not use them as parking spots.* The driver nearest to the passing place should give way to an oncoming vehicle. If you are travelling slowly, pull in to let faster cars overtake. A word of warning: sheep wander slowly up the roads and even lie down on them for a nap.
In remoter areas, fill up with petrol when you can, as petrol stations may be far apart and are likely not be open late or on Sundays.

Electricity
The voltage throughout Scotland is 240 volts, 50 HZ AC. Sockets take three-point, square-pin plugs. If you are visiting from overseas, you will need an adaptor, and maybe a transformer too.

Embassies and Consulates
Most of Scotland's foreign relations are conducted in London, where the embassies are situated, and it is to London that most foreigners will need to refer their problems. The USA, Australia and Canada have consulates in Edinburgh. Australians can call (tel: 0131 555 4500), Americans (tel: 0131 556 8315) and Canadians (tel: 0131 220 4333).

Emergency Telephone Number
The number to remember is 999. You will be asked if you require the police, ambulance or fire brigade. The call is free and can be made from any public phone booth.

Entertainment Information
The fortnightly magazine *The List* has details of what's on and where in Glasgow and Edinburgh. During the festivals in the two cities, almost any newspaper or magazine will be crammed with information, and there are special publications too. In the other cities, and deep in the countryside, a combination of your local tourist office and the hotel reception will be able to advise you on how to plan your day or evening, and keep you informed of local events.

Health

No health certificates are required for visitors to Scotland, nor any inoculations. For emergency illness the National Health Service will treat any citizen of the EU or a visitor from a country with a counterpart health arrangement. Check with your doctor before travel. EU citizens should bring with them an E111 form. Visitors from overseas are strongly recommended to take out comprehensive health insurance.

Holidays (Public and Religious)

Scotland has only one statutory public holiday, New Year on 1 January. The Scots, whole-heartedly celebrate New Year's Eve, known as Hogmanay, and the New Year holiday spreads over two or three days.
The other public holidays, known as bank holidays, are on 2 January (or the Monday after if this falls at a weekend), Good Friday (varies between the end of March and April), Easter Monday (three days after Good Friday), the first and last Monday in May, the first Monday in August, St Andrew's Day on 30 November and Christmas on 25 and 26 December. Bank holidays are precisely that – days when the banks close. Many other institutions continue to function. Varying local holidays are also observed.

Lost Property

Large train stations and all airports have a lost property office. In the case of loss elsewhere, contact the local police station to see if your property has been brought in.

Media

Newspapers

Scotland has its own national press, based in its four largest cities. *The Scotsman* (Edinburgh) and the *Herald* (Glasgow) are genuinely national, while the *Press and Journal* (Aberdeen) and the *Dundee Courier* are more local. Evening newspapers include the *Evening News* (Edinburgh), the *Evening Times* (Glasgow), the *Evening Telegraph and Post* (Dundee) and the *Evening Express* (Aberdeen). The Scottish tabloid, the *Daily Record*, is highly popular. On Sundays the most widely read newspapers are the *Sunday Post* and the *Sunday Mail* with *Scotland on Sunday* filling the broadsheet slot.

Quiet road on the west coast

DIRECTORY

Clydesdale Bank – in Gaelic

All London-based newspapers are available in Scotland, although they may not be stocked in smaller shops, and newsagents in the centre of the major cities will also stock a selection of foreign papers.

Radio
Scotland broadcasts the major UK stations run by the BBC. **Radio 1**, on FM 97.6-99.8MHz, broadcasts pop music to a targeted young audience. **Radio 2**, FM 88-90.2 MHz is for an older age group who like golden oldies, easy listening and friendly talk. **Radio 3**, FM 90.2-92.4MHz, is the classical music channel, while **Radio 4**, LW 198kHz, FM 92.4-94.6MHz, broadcasts current affairs, news, interviews, documentaries, plays and serials. **Radio 5**, MW 909, 693kHz, concentrates on sport, interviews and documentaries. **Radio Scotland** broadcasts on MW 810kHz, FM 92.4-94.7MHz. The BBC **World Service** is found on MW 648kHz, 463m in Scotland. There are numerous commercial radio stations including **Radio Clyde** (Glasgow area) and **Radio Forth** (Edinburgh). There are also local gaelic-speaking services.

Television
Scottish terrestrial television receives four stations, BBC1 and 2, ITV and Channel 4. All show many of the same programmes as are broadcast to the rest of the British Isles, though BBC Scotland and the Scottish ITV regional franchises all make programmes of particular relevance to Scotland, including daily local news bulletins. You will find a few programmes in Gaelic. There are several satellite channels.

Money Matters

There is no restriction on the amount of money, be it in travellers' cheques or cash, that you may bring in to Scotland. You can also freely take Scottish currency away with you.

By and large Scotland shares the decimal currency of the United Kingdom, based on the pound sterling, which is divided into 100 pence. Notes come in five denominations, £50, £20, £10, £5 and £1, the latter being the only anomaly, a note no longer found in the rest of Great Britain. Bank of England notes printed by the Scottish banks are equally common and acceptable. Though some shopkeepers elsewhere in Britain are reluctant to accept Scottish notes, they can always be exchanged in banks without difficulty. You will also become familiar with the following coins: £1, 50p, 20p, 10p, 5p, 2p and 1p. Major credit cards are generally accepted but do not expect every two-table pub to take them.

Opening Times

Banks

Open 09.15–16.00/16.45hrs on weekdays, and many stay open until 17.30hrs on Thursdays. Closed on Saturdays, Sundays and public holidays.

Post Offices

Open Monday to Friday 09.00–17.30hrs and Saturday 09.00–12.30 or 13.00hrs. The smaller post offices (sub-post offices), which are incorporated into the village shop or run in a remote valley, may close for lunch and a half-day on Wednesdays.

Tourist Offices

Open 09.00–18.00hrs, though in rural areas they may have shorter hours and even close down during the winter months.

Museums

Opening times vary widely. Check them individually.

Personal Safety

Scotland is a relatively safe place for tourists. Threatening areas in the major cities are rarely on the tourist track, and apart from a little rowdiness after the pubs close on Friday and Saturday nights, most Scottish towns are usually very quiet.

Pharmacies

These are known in Britain as Chemists. The pharmacist is trained to suggest non-prescription drugs for various ailments. If (s)he feels (s)he cannot deal with your complaint then a local doctor will be recommended.

Places of Worship

The Protestant Church of Scotland has churches throughout the land.

Religion in Scotland has been rife with schisms, and there are a number of smaller, more puritanical congregations who render a few parts of Scotland deathly quiet through their prohibition on doing anything other than studying the Bible on Sundays. If this is to your taste you should head for a service in any church of the Free Church of Scotland.

Catholics will find a healthy smattering of churches across the country. Synagogues and mosques are mainly to be found in Edinburgh and Glasgow.

Police see **Crime** and **Lost Property**

Post Offices
The smallest village in Scotland will have a post office, often attached to the local shop and marked by a distinctive red and yellow sign. Sometimes they are even housed in caravans. Airmail letters should arrive at most destinations well within a week of posting, postcards a little later. You can send national and international telegrams by dialling 0800 190190.

To receive letters poste restante choose at least a medium-sized post office. They will be kept for you for three months, then returned to the sender if you fail to collect them.

Public Transport

Air
Between them, British Airways and British Airways Express (formerly Loganair) provide a network of services between major airports on Scotland's mainland and her often remote island communities. All reservations and enquiries can be dealt with by calling British Airways on 0345 222111.

Buses
Scottish Citylink (tel: 0990 505050) links the major cities in Scotland: Edinburgh, Glasgow,

Aberdeen, Perth, Dundee and Inverness. If for any reason they fail you, call **Caledonian/ National** (tel: 0990 808080). Local bus services connect towns and most villages, though they are often very infrequent and rarely run on Sundays or public holidays. Information can be obtained from local bus stations. In rural areas the **Postbus** (which delivers mail) also carries fare-paying passengers in places reached by no other form of public transport. Timetable from: Royal Mail Public Relations Unit, West Port House, 102 West Port, Edinburgh EH3 9HS (tel: 0131 228 7407).

Trains
Trains are efficient in Scotland and journeys often a pleasure in themselves. Trips especially noted for their beautiful scenery include: Glasgow–Stranraer, Glasgow–Mallaig, Perth–Inverness and Inverness–Kyle of Lochalsh. If you plan to do a lot of rail travel in Scotland it would be worth buying a 'Freedom of Scotland' pass which allows you unlimited travel all over Scotland for 7 or 14 days.

Ferries
The cheapest way of reaching the islands, though still expensive, is by ferry. The **Caledonian MacBrayne Company** has a subsidised monopoly to keep the lines of communication going to these remote communities (tel: 01631 562285). It offers passenger and car ferries, and a series of different fares and routes.

Taxis

Black cabs operate in the major cities and can be hailed with ease. In the countryside, ask your hotel receptionist or a publican to provide you with the telephone number of a local cab company which can be used to book a taxi. Fares are very reasonable away from the big cities.

Senior Citizens

Reductions are available for all senior citizens (with proof of their status) at most museums, cinemas and theatres in Scotland. The elderly are also given concessions on public transport.

Student and Youth Travel

Children aged 5 to 15 travel at a reduced rate on all forms of public transport. It is wise to travel with proof of age if you want to take advantage of cheaper fares. An International Student Identity Card entitles students to reduced travel and entry to museums, theatres and sports events. There are also many youth hostels in Scotland, for which you need an IYHF membership card. For a list write to the **Youth Hostels Association**, Trevelyan House, 8 St Stephens Hill, St Albans, Herts, AL1 2DY. If you are

Post Office, Stockinish, Harris

aged 16 to 25 and plan to use the train a lot, you should purchase a Young Persons Railcard through your travel agent while still at home. It allows you unlimited journeys over a specified length of time. Full-time students over 17 can travel even cheaper with a Student Coach Card available from National Express, who also offer a Young Person's Coach Card (age-limit 16 to 23).

Telephones

British Telecom's endless image-changes mean that in Scotland a telephone box may be anything from an old fashioned red-painted booth to a smoked-glass box embellished with a leaping trumpeter. They will either accept coins (£1, 50p, 20p and 10p) or green phonecards which you can buy at all post offices and many newsagents. Ten pence is the minimum you need to make a phone call. Calls made after 13.00hrs are less expensive and those made after 18.00hrs and at the weekend are cheaper still. For operator services and to find out the relevant international directories number call 100. Local directory enquiries are on 192, and for any other queries dial 191. To phone abroad dial 00 followed by 61 (Australia), 1 (Canada and USA), 33 (France), 49 (Germany), 39 (Italy), 64 (New Zealand), 34 (Spain), followed by the local code (without its initial 0) and then the number.

Be warned not to make international telephone calls from your hotel as a large percentage will be added.

Time

Scotland operates on Greenwich Mean Time (GMT) which is five hours ahead of Eastern Standard Time. From March till October Scotland switches to British Summer Time which is six hours ahead of Eastern Standard Time.

Tipping

Service is included in many hotel and restaurant bills, but if you feel you've been well treated, then you might like to leave a tip. Taxi drivers, hairdressers and waiters should be rewarded for good service with no less than a 10 per cent tip.

Toilets

These are marked either WC or Public Conveniences, and are, of course, divided by sex.

Tourist Offices

Scotland is well served by tourist offices in the towns and many out-of-the-way but scenic locations. The Scottish Tourist Board's national offices in the British Isles are at 23 Ravelston Terrace, Edinburgh EH4 3EU (tel: 0131 332 2433) and 19 Cockspur Street, London SW1Y 5BL (tel: 0171 930 8661/2/3). For information about visiting Scotland outside the United Kingdom, go to your nearest British Tourist Authority. These include one at 551 Fifth Avenue, Suite 701, New York, NY 10176 (tel: 212/986 2266), one at Suite 450, 111 Avenue Road, Toronto, Ontario M5R 3J8 (tel: 416/925 6326) and one at 210 Clarence St, Sydney, NSW 2000 (tel: 2-267 4555).